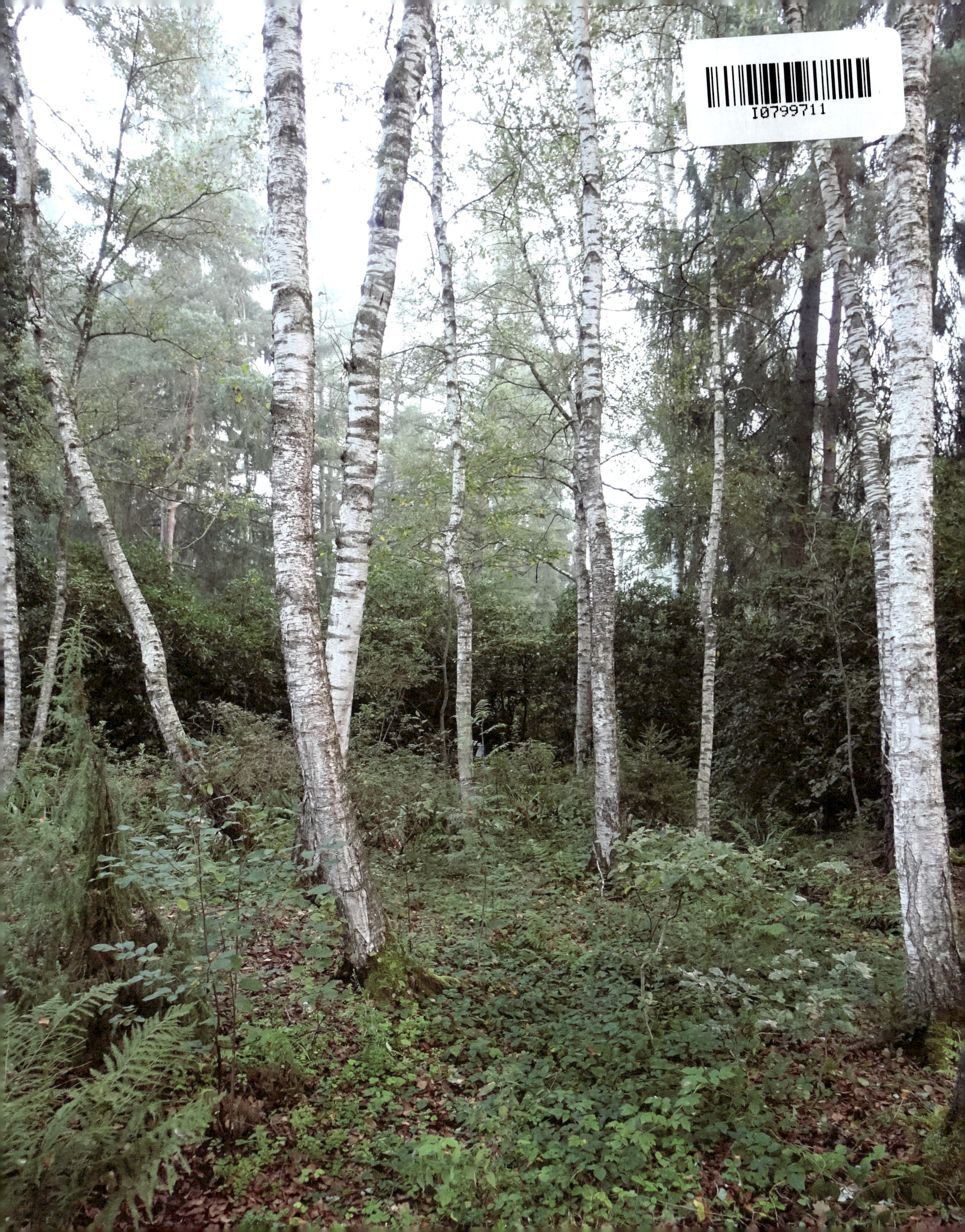

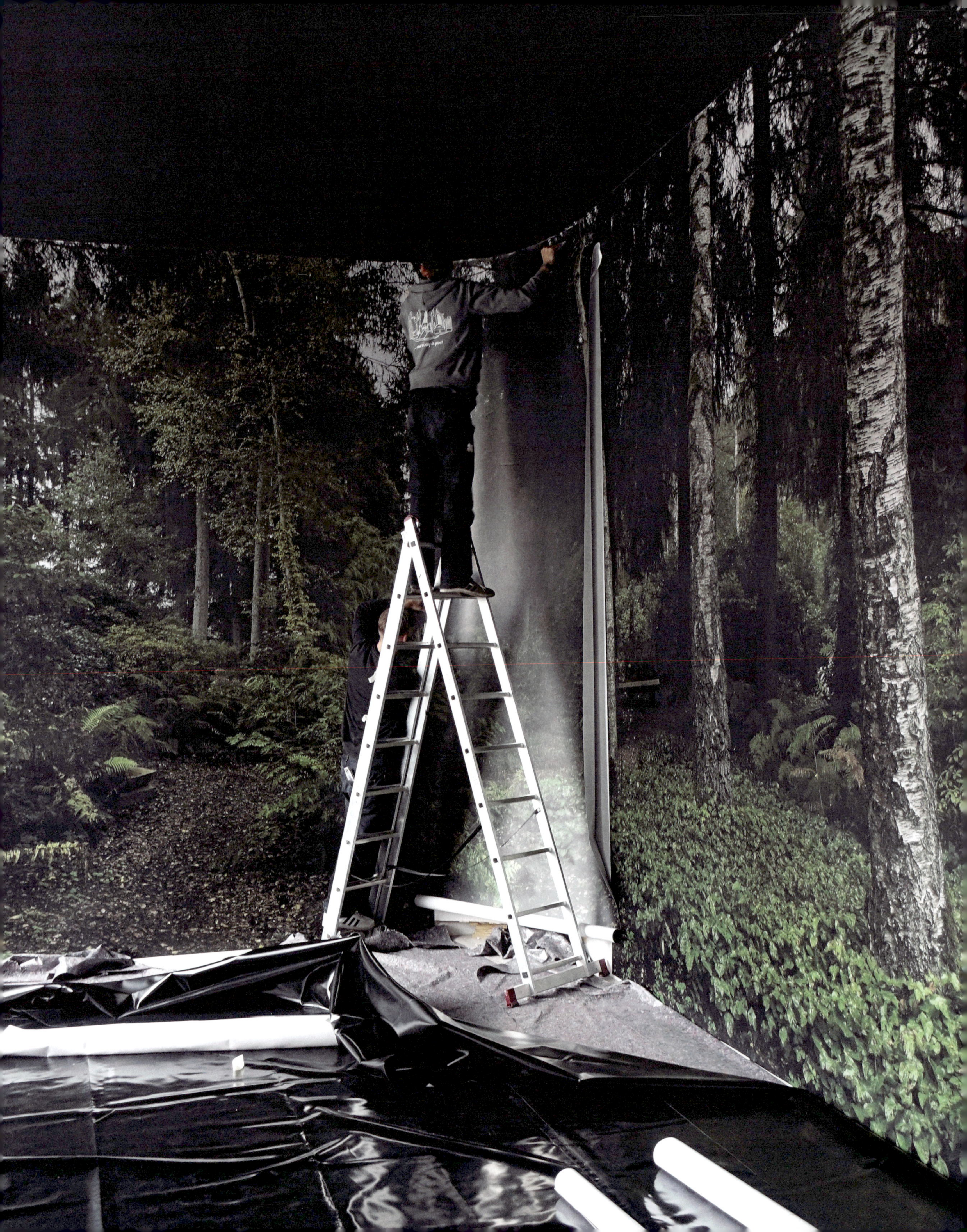

GARDEN

Stephen Bates
Daniel Ganz
Martin Steinmann

Edelaar Mosayebi Inderbitzin

PARK BOOKS

Contents

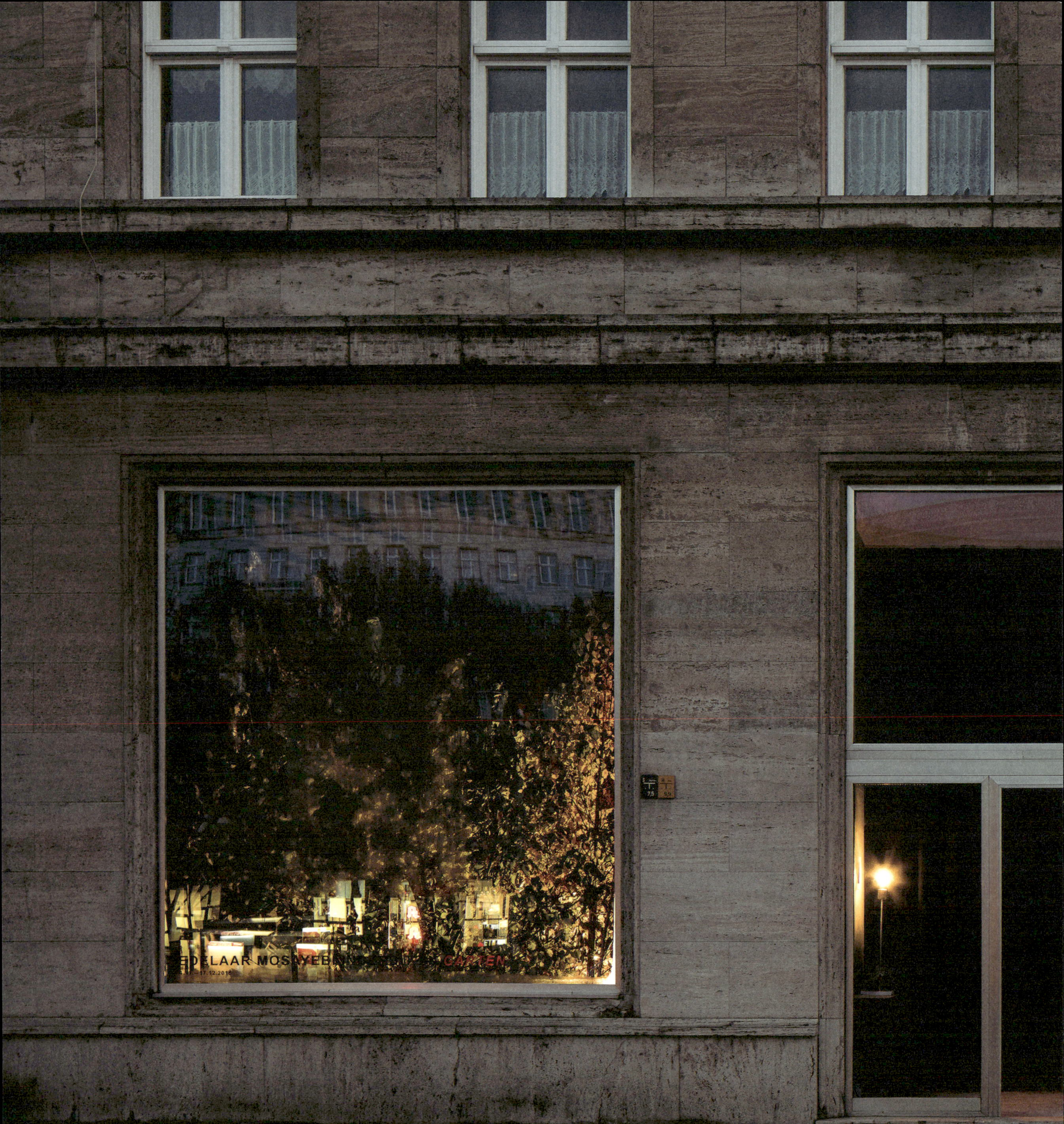
GARTEN

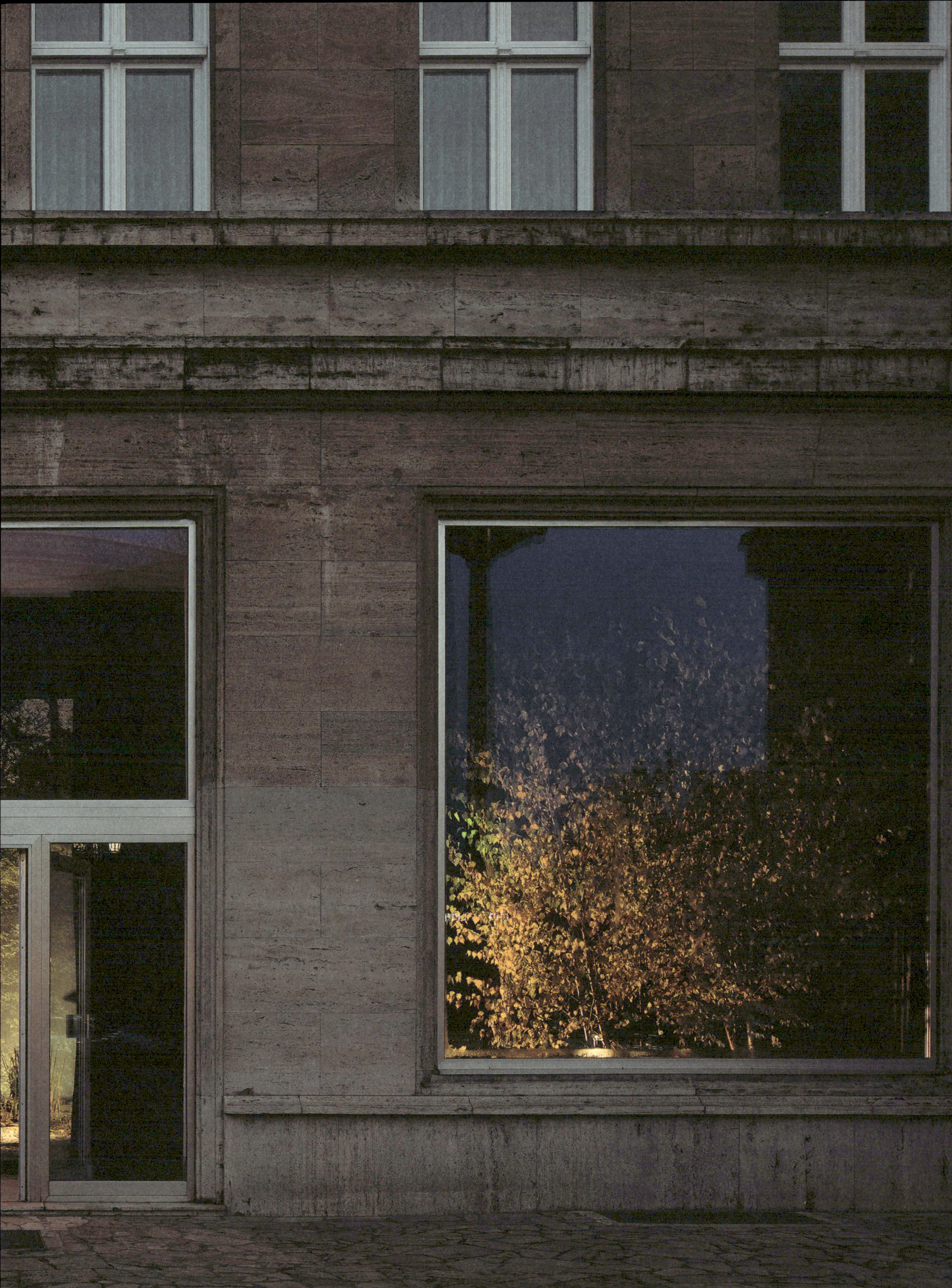

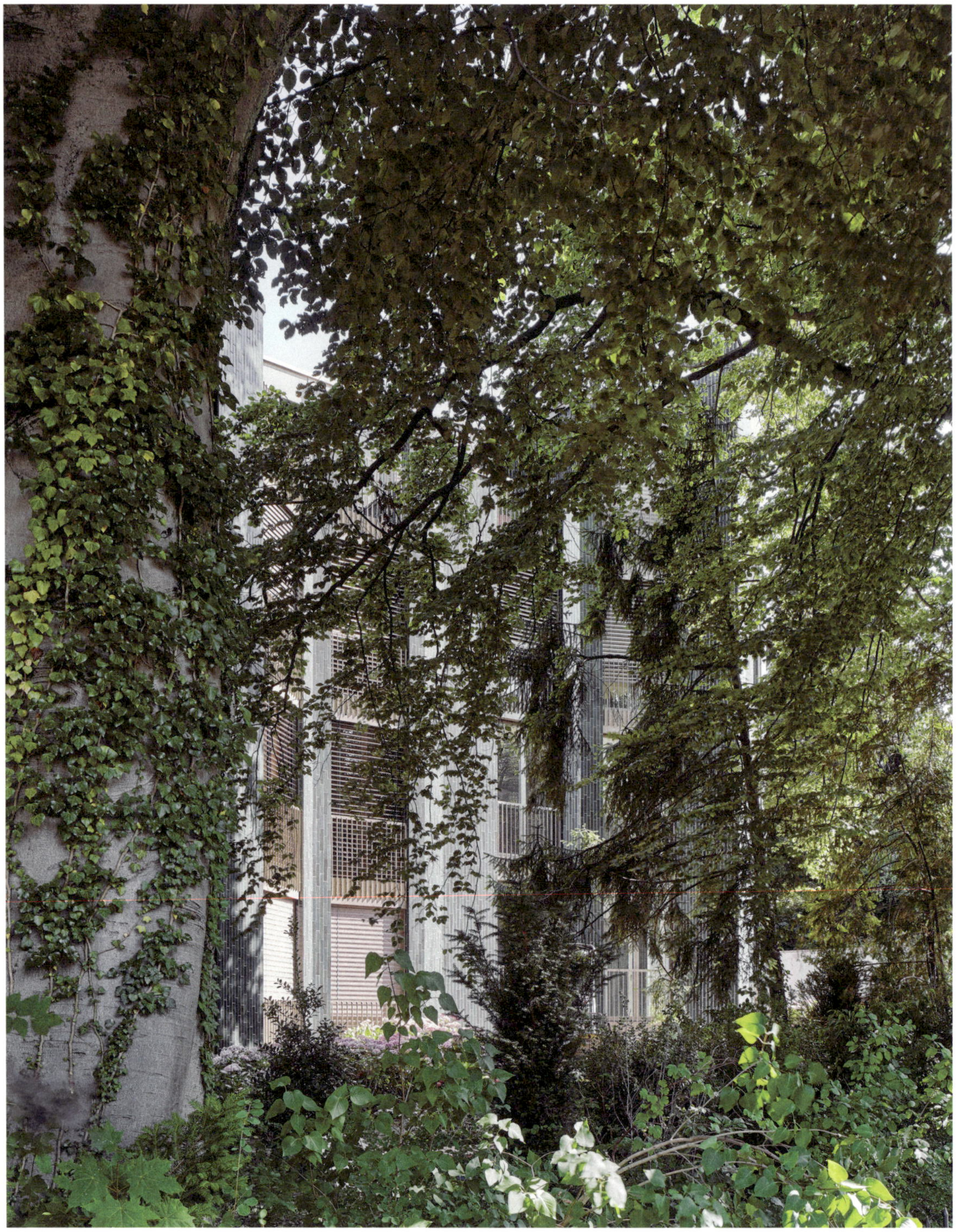

Steinwiesstrasse Residential Development, Zurich-Hottingen

The garden as idea, vision and built space

Gardens have been of great interest in our theoretical work and built projects since our student days. The initial point of departure was the survey and description of the mannerist garden in Bomarzo to the north of Rome. In this garden not far from his castle, Graf Vicino Orsini transformed a wood of oak trees and its rugged boulders into a 'biographical landscape': a bizarre coming-to-terms with personal experiences and extraordinary fantasies. The motif of metamorphosis, influenced by Ovid, determined the emergence and the development of the garden and brought together the elements of nature and art to the point of forging a 'natural work of art'. Basically, everything in nature can thereby become art. Conversely, years of neglect, overgrowth and weathering have not destroyed the enigmatic landscape of the *Sacro Bosco* but actually perfected it. The ruin as a natural work of art *per se* might be said to have anticipated the state of perfection. And so Orsini created 'a mortal image of immortality' (cited in: Ulrich Stadler, 'Bedeutend in jedem Fall: Ein Panorama-Blick auf die Ruinen', in: Assmann, Gomille, Rippl, *Ruinenbilder,* p. 271).

A study trip to England followed, during which we looked into the term and ideational history of the Picturesque, which is closely related to English landscape gardens and landscape painting. The Picturesque was conceptualized in 18th-century England, establishing a third category between the *sublime* and the *beauti-*

ful, which, in simplified terms, integrated the irrational into aesthetic theory and called into question classical ideals of wholeness, purity, harmony and symmetry. However, the Picturesque does not constitute an alternative to the classical ideal of beauty. Rather, it was created as a kind of putty that binds the contradictory, unfinished and fragmentary with the pure and the classical in a self-evident and dialectically open-ended way. This demonstrates the synthetic power of the Picturesque: a loose order established in pictures and perception. Our small publication, *The Picturesque – Synthese im Bildhaften* (2008) represents the attempt to pin down this compositional and design procedure.

Tellingly, our first built project was a home for a gardener. The extremely inexpensive house is a hybrid construction of steel and wood and is distinguished by tectonics and situative details, reminiscent of bricolage. In addition to the direct reference to gardens and the client's nursery, there is also, at least in retrospect, a conceptual link to the ideas associated with gardens, such as Robert Maxwell's notion of the *carefully careless*, which we associate with the informality and openness of the Picturesque. The garden fascinates us as a concept, a body of ideas and a built space.

Our interest in gardens is motivated not least by their affinity with architecture. Gardens, like buildings, refer to the specific place for which they have been designed. At the same time, a garden does not refer exclusively to its immediate surroundings; it also relates to a larger cultural context and an overarching history of ideas. In that respect, the garden creates something new, like every art form, and brings to light things that ordinarily remain hidden. The potential of imagination and idealization, of giving shape to an idea is especially manifest in the garden because it is tied neither to purpose nor to use value (that does not, of course, apply to all gardens). As such, it is a place of longing, a surface of projection and simultaneously an image and a spatial iteration of reality. In addition, gardens are distinctly temporal. While it takes a long time for buildings to age, gardens are, by definition, subject to constant growth and decay. The materials used in gardens are alive: they sprout, grow, bloom and wither. In ruins, the temporality of

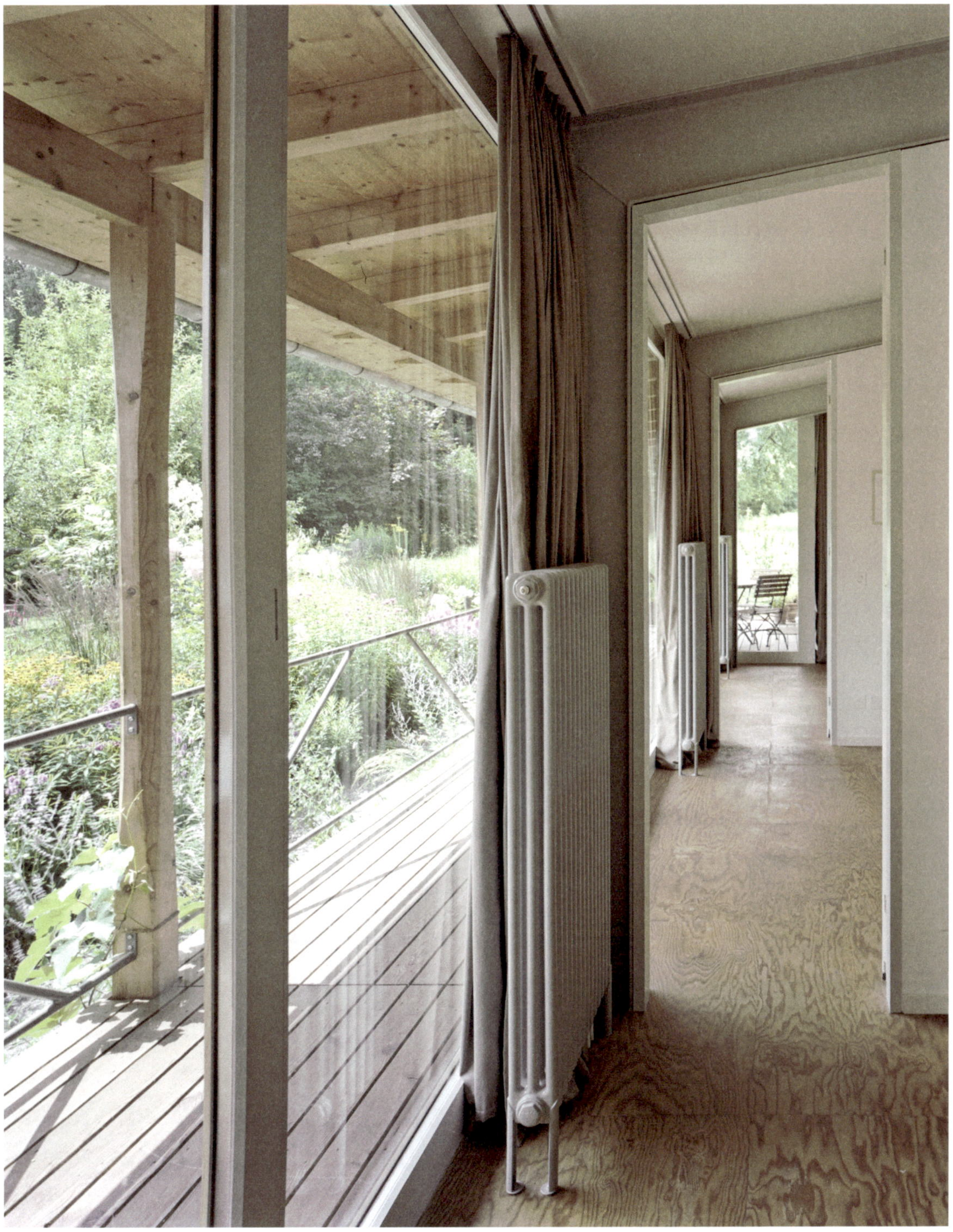

House for a Gardener, Hinterforst

the built environment and nature are synchronous; artefact and vegetation fuse into a new whole. It is therefore no surprise that the ruin has been a recurring motif in the garden arts in various epochs.

The ruin is characterized by a twofold, paradoxical metaphorical imagery. On one hand, it stands for the reconciliation of the difficult and possibly even fraught relationship between nature and culture; on the other hand, it is a fragment of human activity and testifies as such to the presumed loss of wholeness and unity. As a torso, it is a depiction of a fragmentary, disconnected reality. In this respect, our cities have also come to resemble ruins. Despite the beauty of ruins, however, this observation is entirely devoid of nostalgia. As an 'open form', the ruin may even create a field of potential that yields new avenues of action for urban and architectural design.

The ideational world of the garden possesses another reference to the present: The disappearance of the dichotomy between urban and rural has led to a 'total landscape'. Figuratively speaking, Horace Walpole's pithy description of William Kent's radical view of the English landscape might apply: 'He leapt the fence, and saw that all nature was a garden' (Horace Walpole, 'On Modern Gardening', in: Walpole (ed.), *Anecdotes of Painting in England.* Vol. 3, p. 801). Traditional ideas of the city must give way to a new, comprehensive concept of landscape. That landscape will ultimately consist of varying degrees of urbanization. In many places, the customary instrumentarium of urban design will no longer be efficacious so that the landscape approach may well become more cogent.

Gardens and buildings

We are extremely interested in the relationship of architecture and garden in our designs. For us, the term 'garden' is all-embracing and symbolic so that it can also refer to urban space. Ideally, architecture and garden are mutual determinants and linked as an inseparable unity. Initially, the immediate, spatial link of this relationship is foregrounded. In the villa on Signaustrasse in Zurich, built by Pfleghard and Häfeli in 1912, this unity was dismantled by building parking spaces and destroying the garden. Designed by Gustav Ammann, then still working as an employee, the garden marked the transition from the landscaped house garden to the architectural garden. The renovation includes reinstalling the garden, whose content relates to the architectural garden and thus restores the original significance of the building.

A similarly concrete, spatial relationship – in this case on an urban scale – characterizes some of our buildings in Zurich's garden cities. These largely bear the stamp of Zurich's municipal architect Albert Heinrich Steiner, active in the 1940s and 1950s. These projects, the ongoing urban transformation of the neighbourhoods, are matched atmospherically through the choice of construction and materials. The outcome of the competition for the Brüggliäcker Residential Development was decisively influenced through building height restriction to three storeys, ensuring the closeness to the ground that typifies living in that location. The painted wood façade lies behind slender loggias of in-situ concrete. These create great porosity between inside and outside and anchor the building in the garden city of Zurich-Schwamendingen. The three-storey restriction also played a significant role in the urban treatment of the Obsthalde project in Zurich-Affoltern. The simple masonry buildings – the façades consist of single-brick walls plastered on both sides – embody the architectural expression of naïveté and modesty characteristic of garden city architecture in the 1930s and 1940s. The three row-buildings have a foundation, a roof, gutters, waterspouts, etc.

The reinterpretation of the urban situation and the relationship between building and outside space are more pronounced in the projects Am Katzenbach and Schwamendinger Dreieck. Since the Am Katzenbach neighbourhood is completely new, it seemed obvious to differentiate the urban structure of parallel 'strips'.

The new buildings in phase III complete the development facing the slope with its patchwork of existing buildings through a morphological correspondence and housing in the garden, while the new buildings in phases IV and V describe an urban edge and living in the park through transition to the Katzenbach Park. In keeping with this intent, this phase of the project has been designed with the sculptural appearance and materials of city apartment buildings. In contrast, the buildings of phase III with their light corrugated cladding and protruding balconies blend into the purlieus of the surrounding garden vegetation. The affinity with the garden is also expressed in artist Christian Hörler's three reliefs on the foundation, which reference paradise as an everlasting utopia and a present-day haven. In the outdoor spaces of phases IV and V, not only cross-references but also diagonal views of the park from the street are ensured by the polygonal ground plans as adaptations of variations in the depths of the lots. The spaces in between continuously open and close 'softly', a motif borrowed from the landscape park.

The substantial increase in density of the cooperative housing at Schwamendinger Dreieck requires a redefinition of the space. The slender, five-storey buildings are longer and taller than the existing ones. Above the flat S-shape in the ground plan, buildings are placed in tension and shortened depending on standpoint. The mirrored placement of the buildings in relation to each other generates narrow and wide outdoor spaces, which are thereby modulated. In particular through this modulation, the characteristics of the garden city are not negated, but rather given a new form.

The enmeshment of 'unbuilt' outdoor space and the 'built' space of the buildings is also the crucial urban concern in the Toblerstrasse Residential Development. The surrounding buildings at Zurichberg consist largely of single structures on smaller pieces of land with a tight fabric of private garden spaces between them. The project with its compact individual buildings builds on the morphology of the situation and, at the same time, creates a communal outside space for the cooperative through a cabinet of single garden spaces. A kind of balance in the spatial impact of the design exists between the buildings and the empty volumes

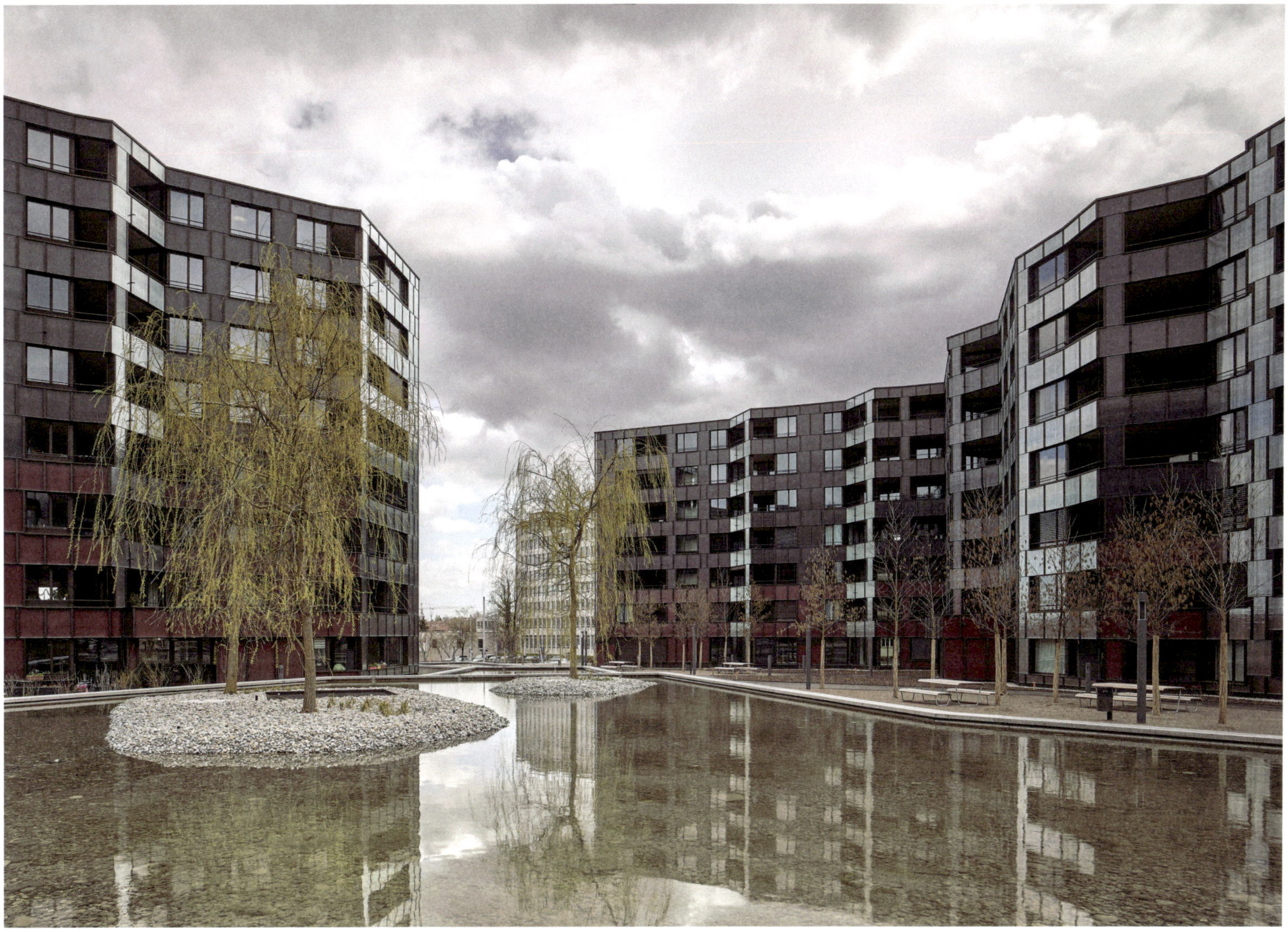

Guggach Residential Development, Zurich

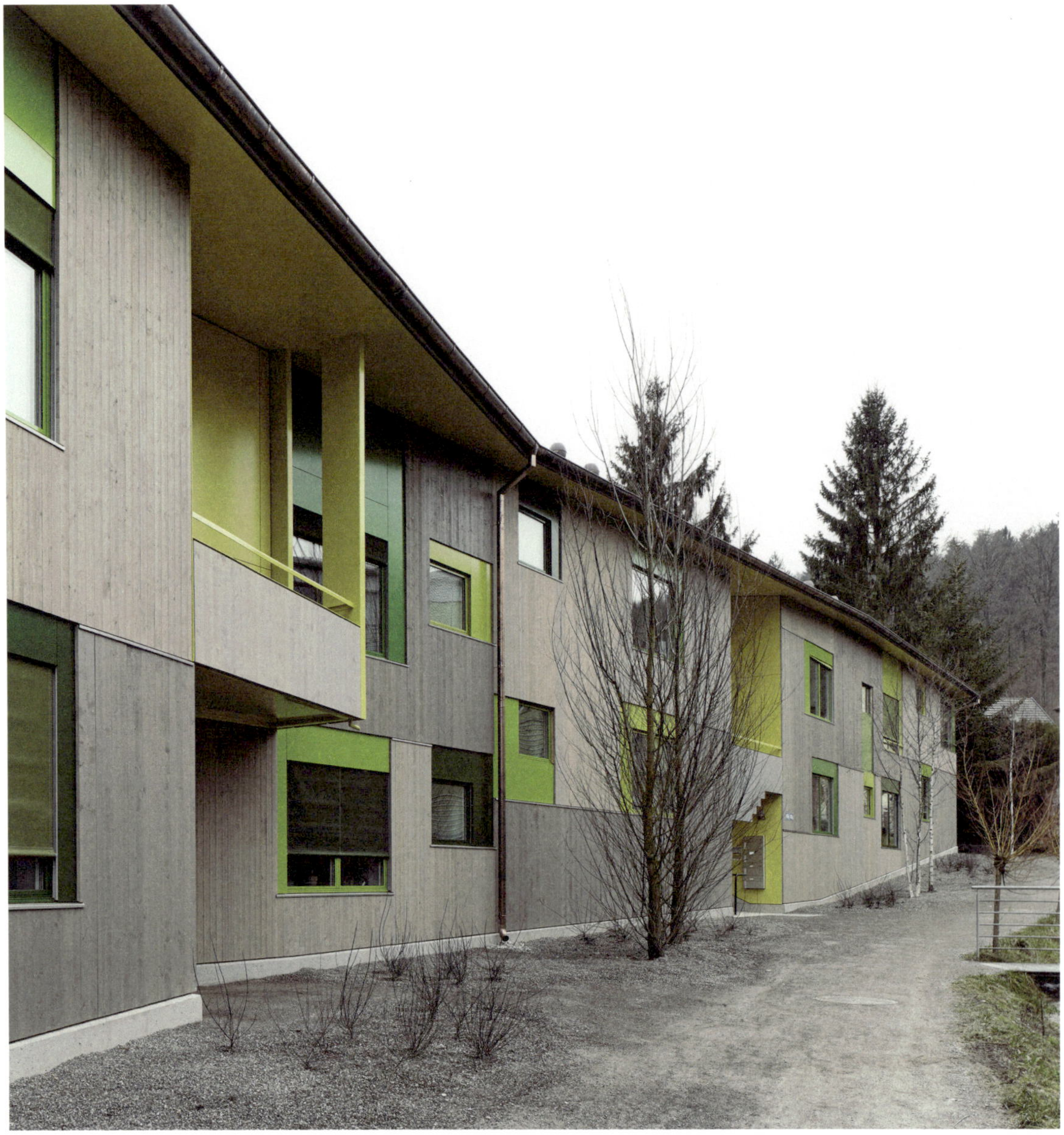

Avellana Residential Development, Zurich-Schwamendingen

of the cabinet. The concave sections of the façade embrace the garden spaces, resembling Baroque arrangements of space, such as that seen at the Piazza San Ignazio in Rome.

The theme of landscape and garden acquires in turn more concrete significance in the Speich Areal, a combined commercial and residential building in Zurich-Wipkingen. The complex urban setting of the project is defined by a busy city street on one side and an open space facing the river landscape of the Limmat on the other. The head of the building faces Wipkingerplatz and the Hardbrücke urban freeway. There, its presence is underscored by a strong sculptural volumetry, while the side facing the river is layered. Terraces lend the urban riverscape of the Limmat successively cultivated layers of vegetation. The river vegetation merges into a vertical garden, which culminates in trellises on the roof terrace. Daniel Ganz's choice of plants, specifically fig and palm trees, resonates with the Mediterranean microclimate of the south-facing river.

In the Guggach Residential Development, centrally located in the saddle between downtown Zurich and Nordstadt, the design of the outdoor environs is determined by architectural principles rather than the adjoining woods. The intention was to add a third, artificial and urban quality to the open spaces of the woods and nearby Brunnenhof estate. The defining feature of the space between the two bracketing buildings are large, polygonal surfaces of water, framed all around by concrete. The reflections of the sky and the buildings in the water are echoed in the modulated cast glass façade. They, too, oscillate between closure and impressions of dematerialization. The combined reflections in the water and in the heavy glass create a framed urban space.

While the projects discussed so far primarily address the relationship between building and outdoor environs, in other words, the built garden, additional aspects are involved in the design and shape of other projects, such as the commercial and residential building Glattpark, the White Building, and the Avellana and Steinwiesstrasse Residential Developments. Here the ideational history of gardens and landscape design figure as a source for the production of architectural meaning and ideas.

The idea of a stone garden underlies the architectural fragments of in-situ concrete in the courtyard of the MIN MAX commercial and residential building in Zurich Nord. The courtyard, its large-format panels also of in-situ concrete, accommodates a large table, a flat basin of water and skylights. The verticals consist of the lift shaft, a support with girders on both sides and a free-form column bearing the courtyard tower. On reaching the top, the column transmutes into the trunk of a ginkgo tree, the only vegetation in the courtyard. The individual elements of this spatial composition each have considerable autonomy and relate to each other very loosely, if at all. They recall the fragments Poliphilo encounters on wandering through landscapes of ruins in his dreams (Francesco Colonna, *Hypnerotomachia Poliphili,* 1499). The notion of the ruin is overlaid with the technological appearance of the ventilation shafts, which are also lent sculptural expression, and the glazing of the courtyard tower.

The terms landscape, horizon and sky are metaphors that describe the interior of the White House in Männedorf, a small, new one-family home. The house has two storeys, the ground-floor related to the garden and the second floor with a view into the distance across the Lake of Zurich. The rooms on both storeys vary in height with horizontal flooring in between, forming the horizon of the house, as it were. The differences in the garden level are the result of height offsets in the platform floor. They are linked via single steps, forming an inner topography or, as said, a landscape. The height of the rooms on the second storey match the silhouette of the roof. The 'sky' of the rooms varies depending on their significance, as does the materialization of the ceilings.

Structural features of the 'garden' were also transferred to the architecture in the Avellana Residential Development, specifically the characteristics of spontaneous growth, chance and formlessness, which are expressed in the composition of the volume, the eaves and gables, the placement of the windows and the colour-

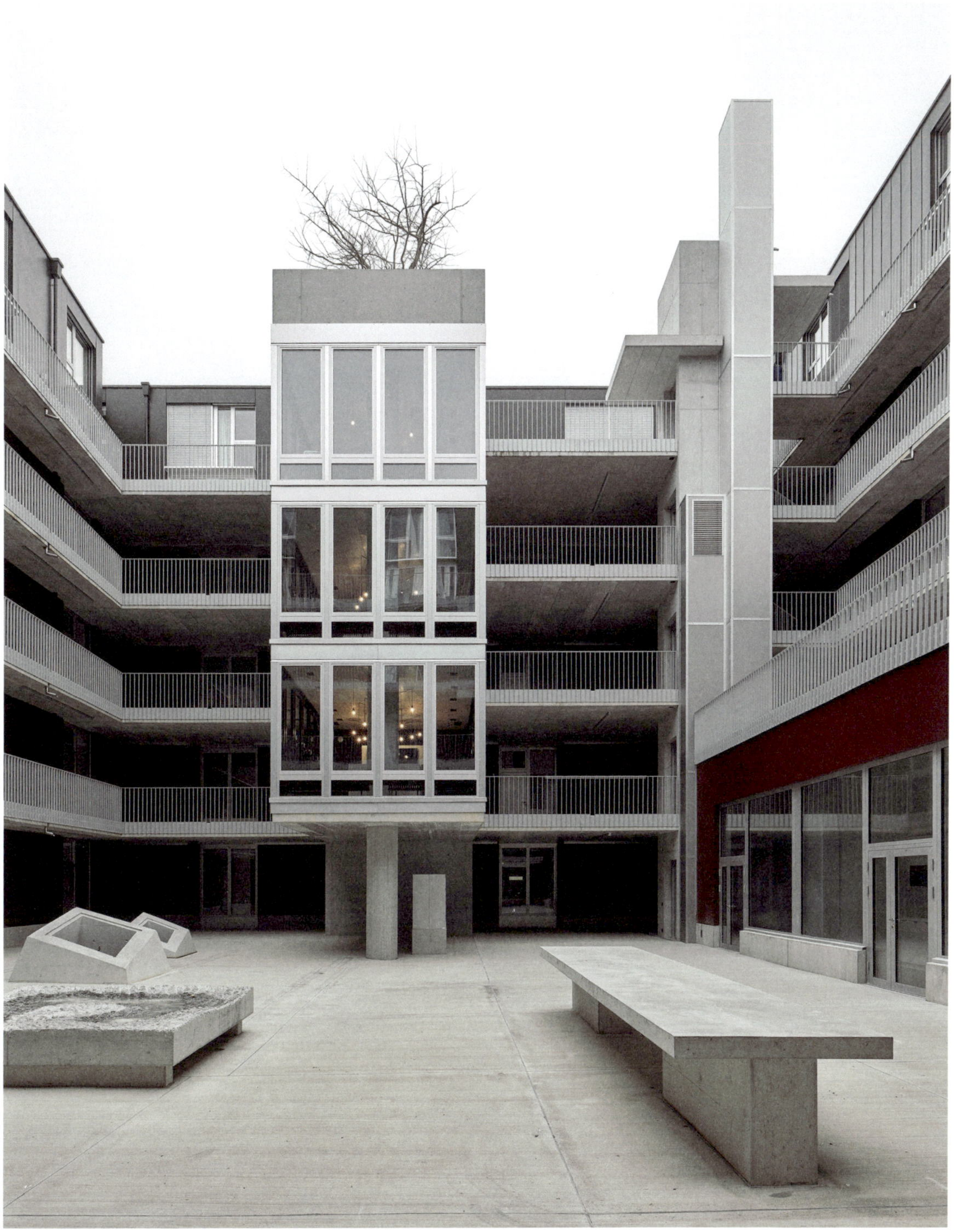

MIN MAX Mixed-Use Residential and Commercial Building, Glattpark, Opfikon

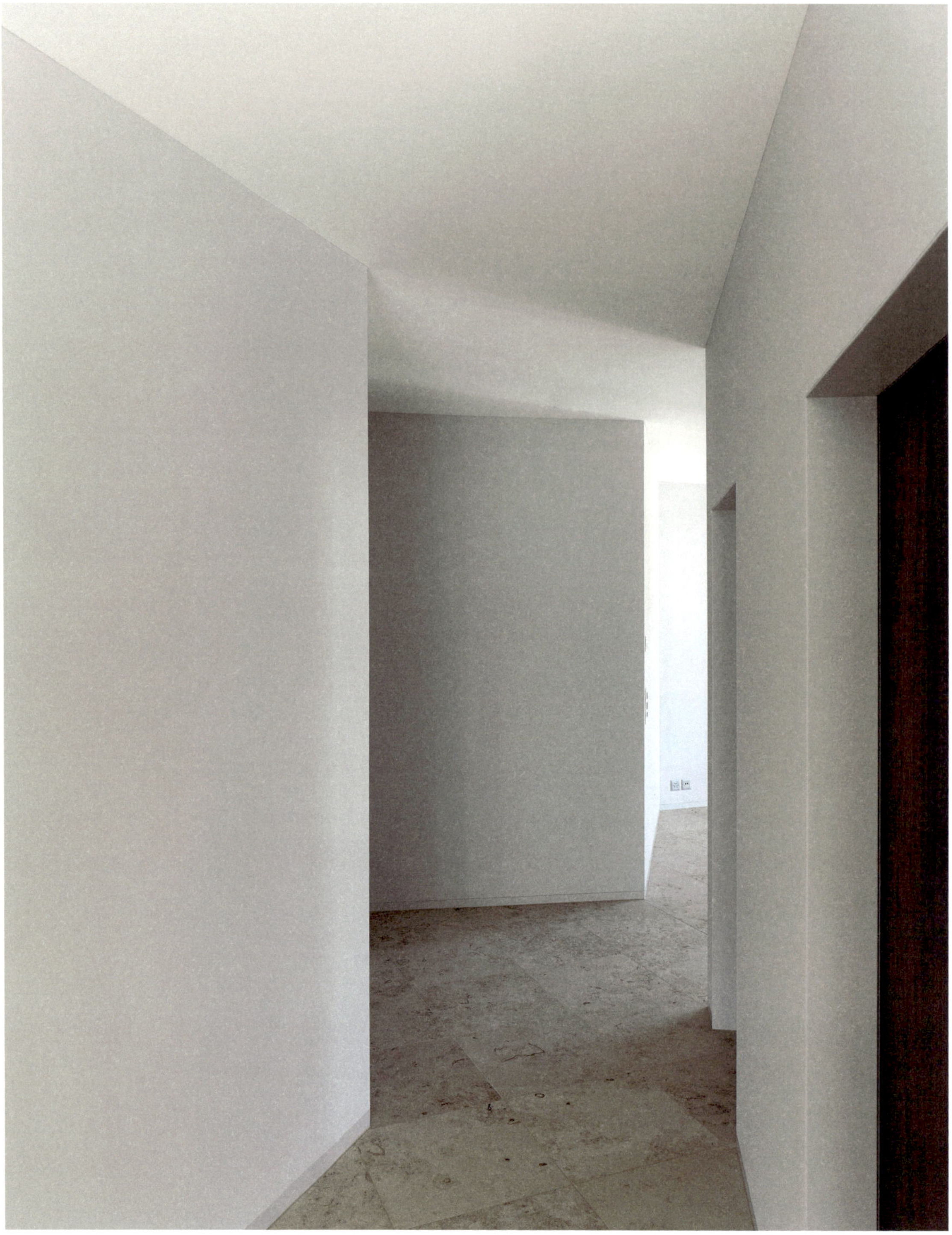

Steinwiesstrasse Residential Development, Zurich-Hottingen

ing of the façades. The architecture of the building references the condition of the garden, prior to developing the parcel, specifically the informality of the place, which was formerly a fallow garden with a few sheds.

Finally, the housing on Steinwiesstrasse in Zurich-Hottingen refers to the relationship between building and garden on several levels. The point of departure was an old, protected stand of trees, framing the parcel along the street and requiring placement of the building in the middle of the parcel. Given the fact that the villas in the neighbourhood are ordinarily placed in this position, the aim was to design a building that withdraws from the context morphologically and typologically, establishing its own specific relationship to the situation. The design was guided by research into forms, specifically the analysis of natural shapes, in particular rock formations such as basalt, which led to an architecture that makes the mighty trunks of the trees a determining element. The composition of the volume and the design of the ground plan feature picturesque principles that obey a situative logic. The building is placed among the trees multidimensionally and cannot be taken in as a whole from any one side – it is, in a sense, shapeless.

A path, as a theme running through the flats, conducts the residents from 'inside' to 'outside', with the fireplace in the living room functioning as a vanishing point of that movement. The unfolding of the rooms within this movement resembles a sequence of scenes, like those featured in landscape gardens. The walls that guide the movement frame various views of the garden and link it to the interior. Because of the varying height offsets of the flats, made possible by direct access from the lift, the eaves do not form a consecutive line. Integrated into the volume as a whole, the top floor thus appears as an 'erosive' factor in the overall form, once again referencing the metaphor of a ruin. And the pillar-like wall sections, glazed in dark green ceramic, generate an architectural expression that can be read as abstract, with an emphasis on materials, and also as pictorial. The pictorial qualities are derived from imitating the surrounding foliage that shimmers in the sunlight.

The garden as a space of illusion and resonance

The garden is a recurring motif in our projects: it may serve as a space of resonance in the design process, as a place of longing or as a source of motif. We took advantage of the opportunity to mount a show at the Architektur Galerie Berlin to develop a self-contained, new project that foregrounds the garden instead of the architecture. For the duration of the exhibition, the gallery was transformed into a living garden: trees, bushes, blossoms, a pond, moss covered stones, weathered benches, chirping birds, the sound of the wind and the smell of wet earth, foliage and rotten wood converged to generate an impressive, intense spatial experience.

For once, it was not about putting a building in a garden but rather about putting a garden in a building. This reversal and alienation frames the topos of the garden and presents its singular value. On one hand, the garden stands for itself; on the other, it addresses a specific interest. The installation explicitly addressed the relationship between architecture and garden, culture and nature, inside and outside. Finally, the appeal of the project lay in rising to the challenge of implementing our intent: how can we manage a deceptively real imitation of a grown garden? Where and how does one draw a line between illusion and reality?

Stephen Bates
Introduction to the exhibition

I've been asked to say a few words by way of an introduction to this remarkable exhibition and installation. I think I was asked not only as a colleague who identifies with the work of Edelaar Mosayebi Inderbitzin Architekten but also because of my connection to a particular cultural phenomenon – a particularly English one – 'the Picturesque' that I believe lies at the heart of Edelaar Mosayebi Inderbitzin's interest in architecture and landscape, and indeed played a part in our meeting in the first place, in London back in 2005.

I don't intend this to be a history lesson but it seems important to create a setting for this installation and for the thinking and making of a certain kind of architectural production.

The Picturesque

The Picturesque – this man-made state of naturalness – emerged in the early eighteenth century as a kind of opposition to French Rationalism and its passion for science and man's intellect and its manipulation of the landscape, as seen in the formal gardens of aristocratic houses. Against such formalism, the Picturesque embraced the ideals of Romanticism. This attempt to integrate cultural ideas of art and narrative was most evident in English architecture through the eighteenth and nineteenth centuries.

Figures like Lord Burlington became interested in the way the design and making of the landscape could enter into a higher cultural discourse. They enjoyed the image of living poetically within the landscape and were inspired in part by the paintings of the French artists Claude and Poussin. The country estate at Petworth, laid out by Capability Brown in the 1790s, explored this idea of setting the house within a naturalized landscape where topography and planting are manipulated to give composed views from the interior and create rich spatial relationships which would be discovered whilst walking. Creating an emotional experience and a specific atmosphere became the most important ambition of these landscape designers.

Unlike the earlier paintings that had been an original influence, these landscapes and their presentation were not dependent on mythical narratives or classical allegories; they became more representative of their owners and celebrated their personal connection to the land.

The sensibility and specificity of designers like Capability Brown and Humphrey Repton came to influence the architects of the Arts and Crafts Movement in the mid-nineteenth century. The work of Philip Webb, and others of this movement, was promoted by Hermann Muthesius in his *Das Englische Haus* of 1904 which gave the movement a greater outreach within the German speaking countries of Europe. Muthesius is widely regarded as a key influence on the development of European architecture, not only through his role as chairman of the Deutsche Werkbund between 1910 and 1916 but also through his involvement in the foundation of Germany's first garden city at Hellerau, near Dresden, in 1909. Here Muthesius promoted the idea that the house and garden could be spatially and atmospherically related, giving it something of the social role of the English landscape tradition, but at a scale that was appropriate to a democratic, middle class society.

The ideas of the Arts and Crafts Movement went on to influence Adolf Loos and Josef Frank, who explored the psychological 'effect' and perception of space in their work. Their interiors of rich spatial plans made obvious links to the experience of landscape, while also seeking comfort and propriety.

Character and interior

Mackay Hugh Baillie Scott (a third generation Arts and Crafts architect and a contemporary of Voysey) was an important influence for Loos and even more so for Frank. In his writings and designs for the 'artistic house' Scott advocated that the house and garden should become a continuum, the house finding its place within a structure of sheltered outdoor spaces and the garden as an extension of the house interior. His book *Houses and Gardens* of 1906 (which was the inspiration for 'Haus und Garten', the company Frank went on to establish) and his 'hall house' plan with its interplay of small, intimate spaces against the larger volume of the hall, inspired Frank in the rich spatial planning of his Villa Beer of 1930 and the important text that followed in 1931, 'Das Haus als Weg und Platz' (The House as Path and Place).

Scott, like Loos and Frank, was looking for character in the making of rooms and spaces. He described his aim to make houses of a 'still, quiet earnestness which seems to lull and soothe the spirit with promises of peace' (M.H. Baillie Scott, *Houses and Gardens,* p. 39).

Something we can all aim for, perhaps …

I find the idea of the 'carefully careless' – a kind of studied tolerance where control is not the overriding principle, but rather a careful organization of space and composition of elements – gives the impression of a more organic, 'as found' character.

City

So we see the emerging connection between a landscape sensibility and an interest in the everyday and in phenomenology. In the 1960s, some artists became interested in 'as found' settings, among them Fischli/Weiss with their photographs of the suburbs of Zurich captured with open eyes and without irony. Buildings, road markings, trees – all these background elements make up the atmosphere of normality while revealing its latent energy and potential. This transfer of picturesque ideas from the countryside to the urban and suburban setting is an important step in its evolution, as it invites a sensitive approach to the everyday and to life as lived in the city.

This sensibility to the role of landscape and the garden retains a pertinence, a usefulness, despite the reality of the ever decreasing scope of the public realm in our cities and the reduction in green spaces, under threat from economic pressure on most projects where the landscape budget is often the first to be compromised.

Perhaps we should see a positive trait in Zurich where, increasingly, competitions for housing developments require the inclusion of a landscape architect on any architectural team. It is clear that Edelaar Mosayebi Inderbitzin Architekten take their collaborations with landscape architects very seriously. The installation here is the product of a continuing collaboration with landscape architect Daniel Ganz, who was involved in Hottingen and Speich among other projects.

Garden

This knowledge, this sensibility, is present in the work of Ron Edelaar, Elli Mosayebi and Christian Inderbitzin – in the way that they approach projects – and it underlies the installation we see before us. The experience is both spatial and sensual. It comprises soft growing things and mud. It is studied, composed and in a way controlled, but it celebrates the natural and the tolerant. It seeks a kind of beauty and it places experience at its heart.

I think it holds a message for us and perhaps for the authors themselves: when we design architecture and interiors, the garden can teach us to cultivate the controlled naturalness of the thinkers of the Picturesque, to consider the democratization of spaces, to allow for change, to be willing to make spaces which may have an underlying functional promise but are open to use and interpretation. And to have character and not be banal –

which I find particularly useful and provocative in the context of current Swiss architectural culture and production.

And so I invite you to experience this rich and intimate landscape, but to do so in the awareness that in its making lies the motivation to make meaningful architectural space. Consider it when you study their work – urban work – that is seeking to eke out and protect or preserve vital green spaces between things, spaces rich with fragrances that stimulate memory, spaces that through their physicality draw our attention back to our body, and which ultimately satisfy the heart.

Berlin, 3 November 2016

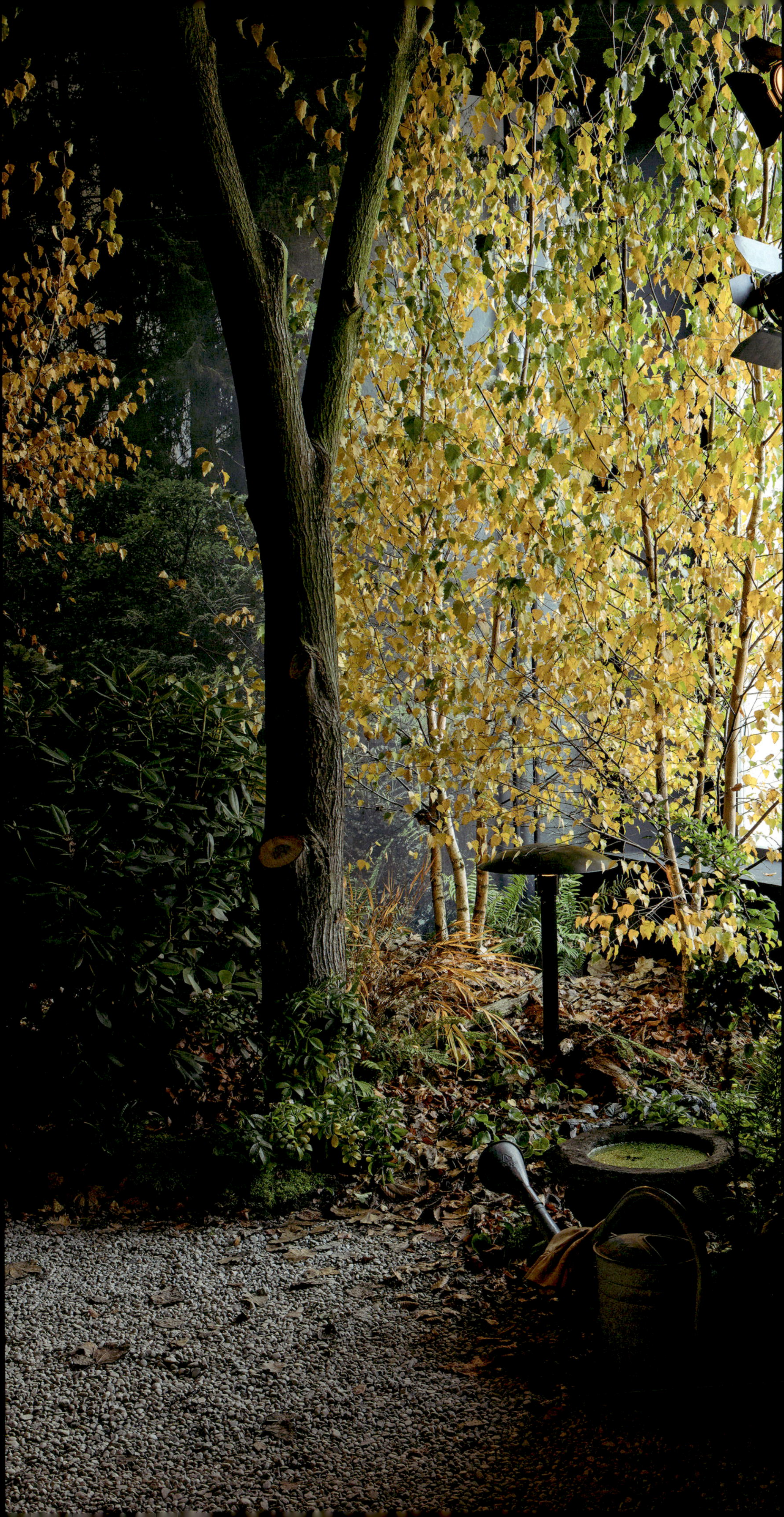

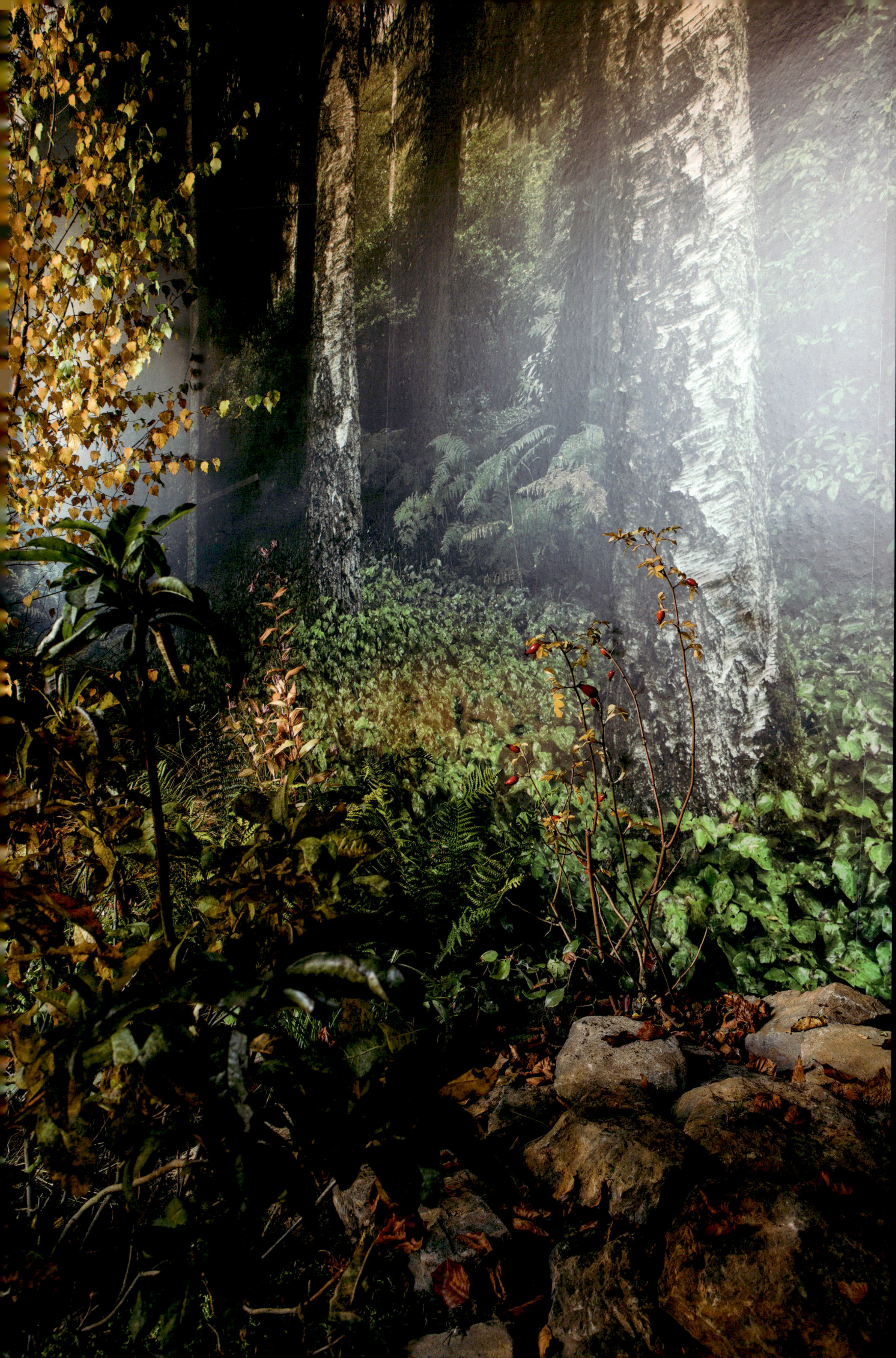

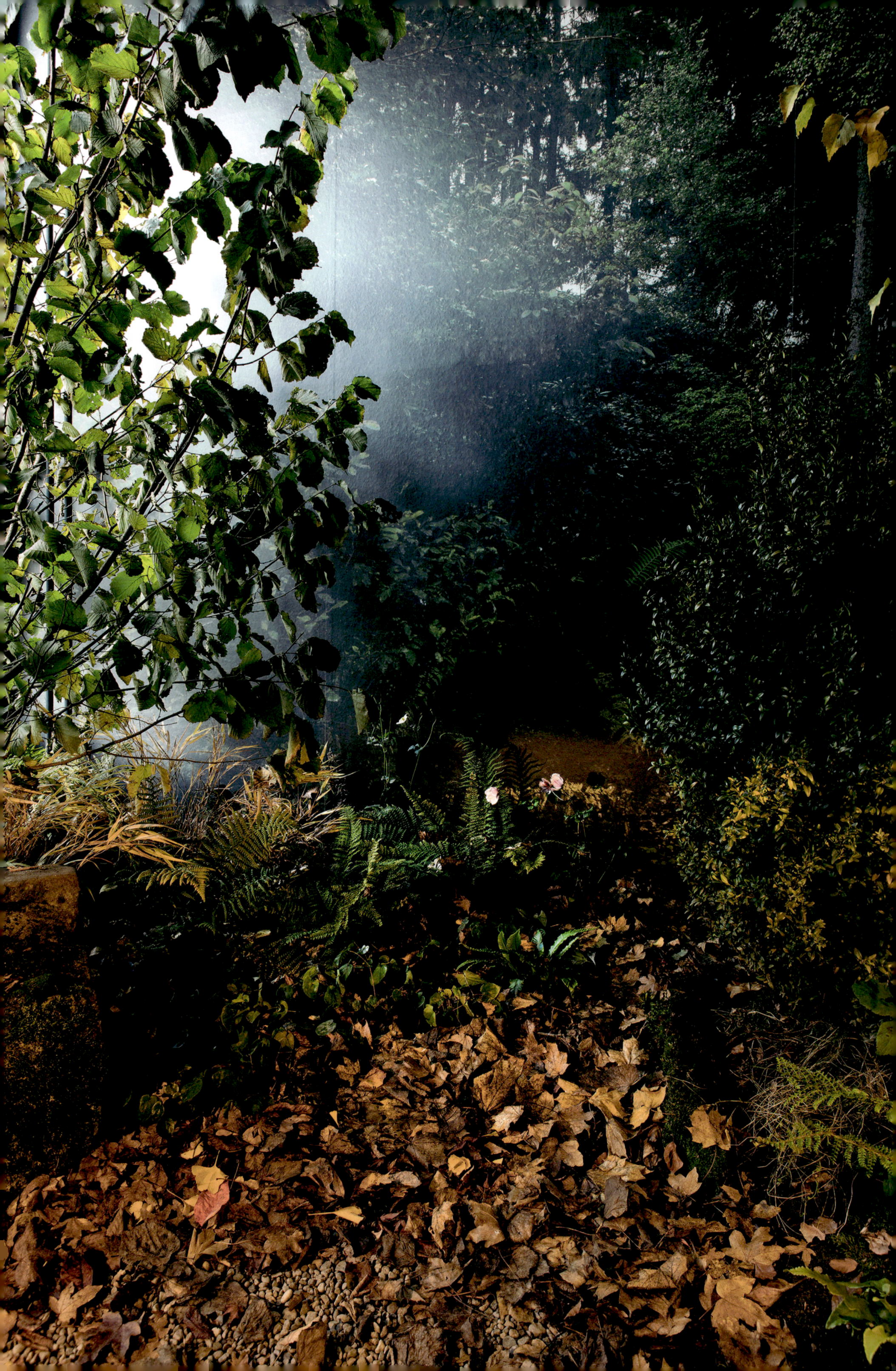

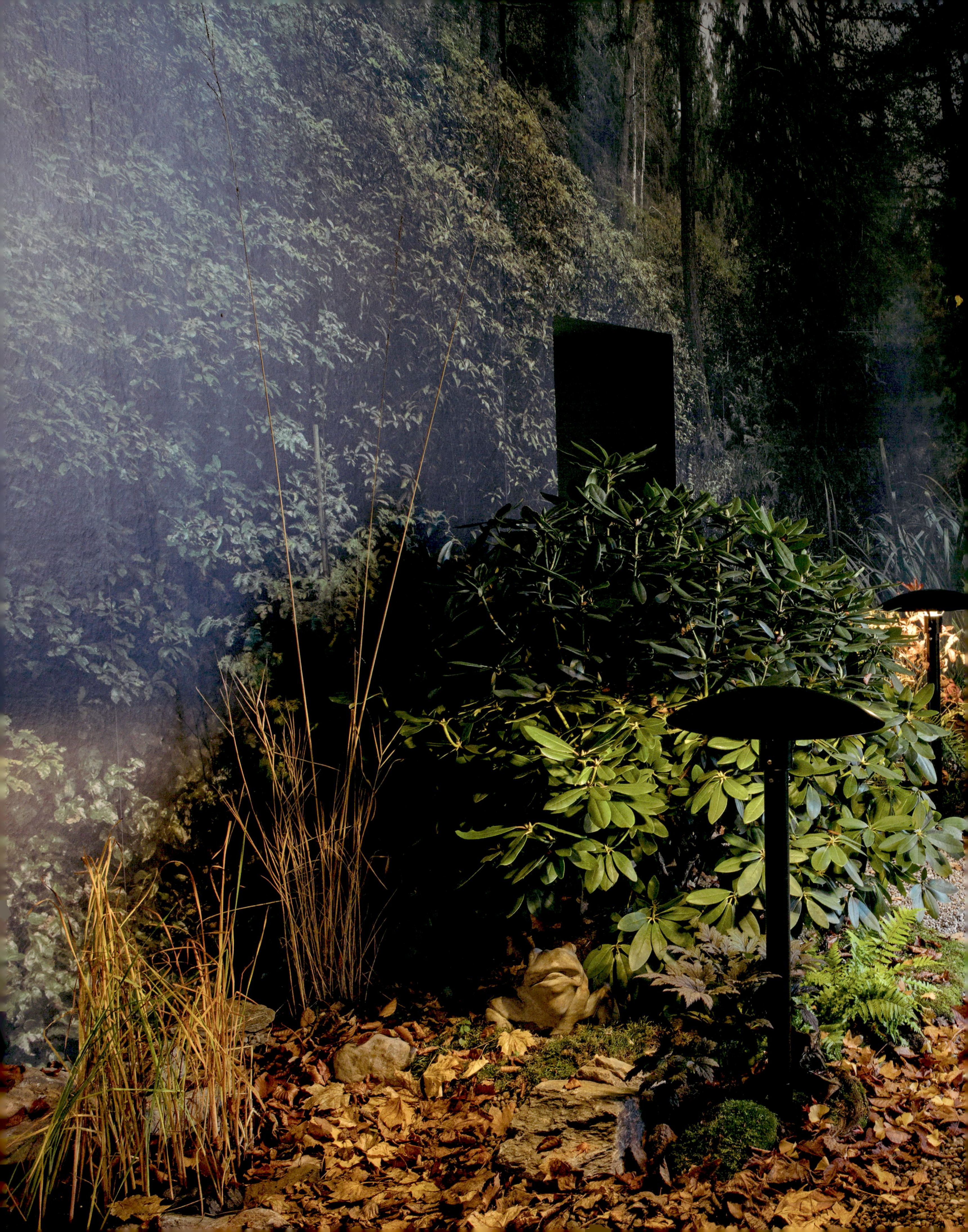

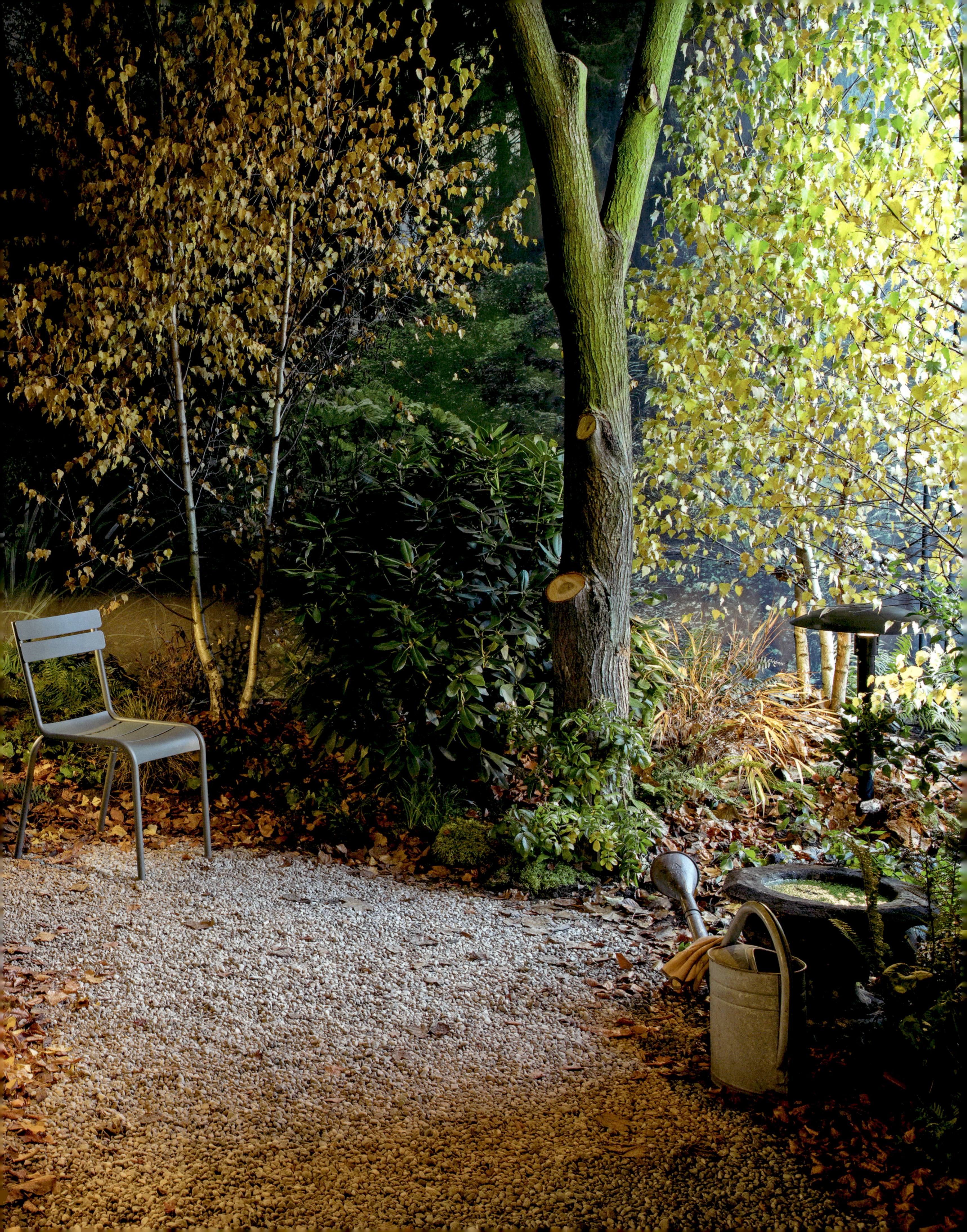

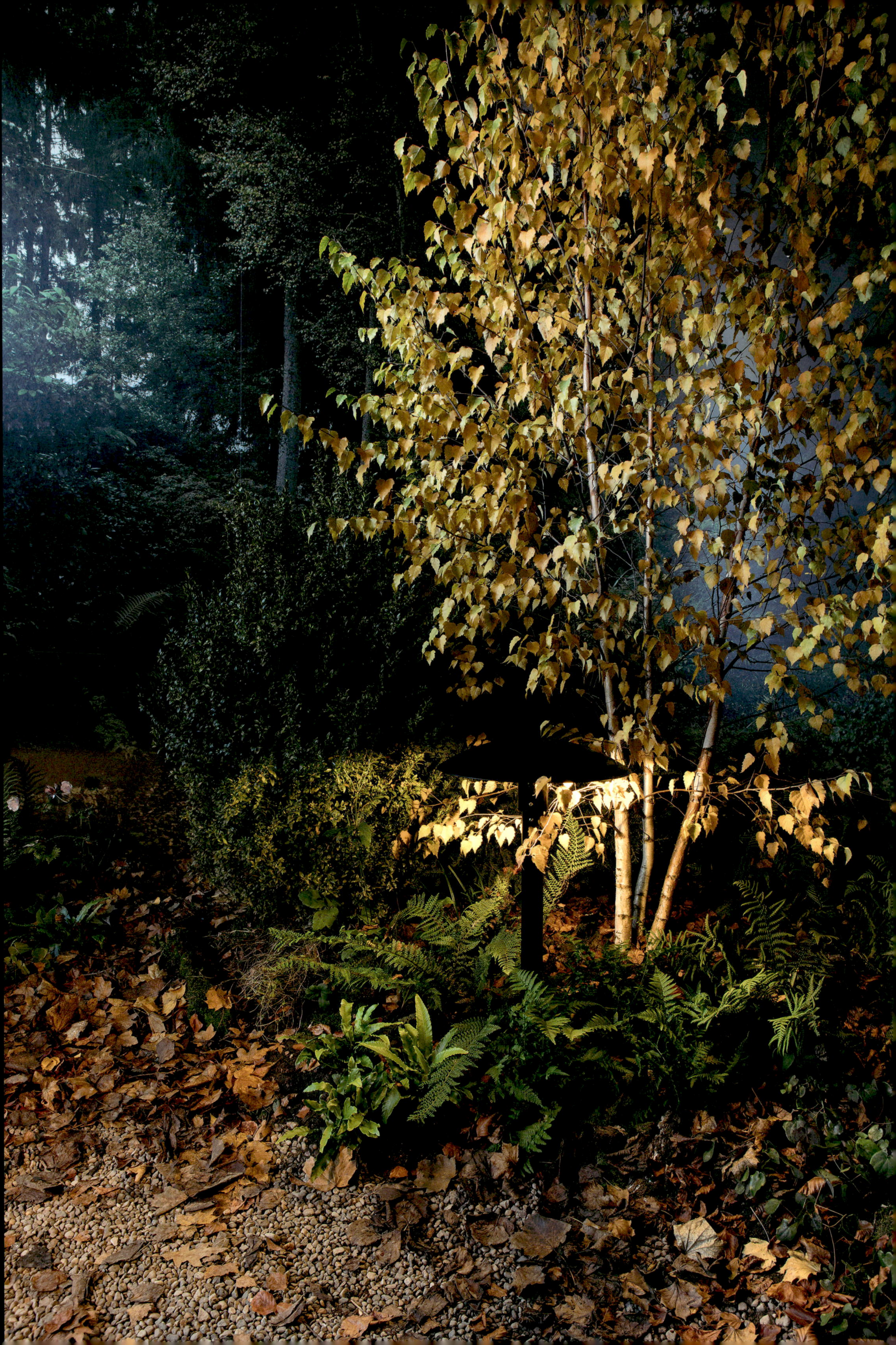

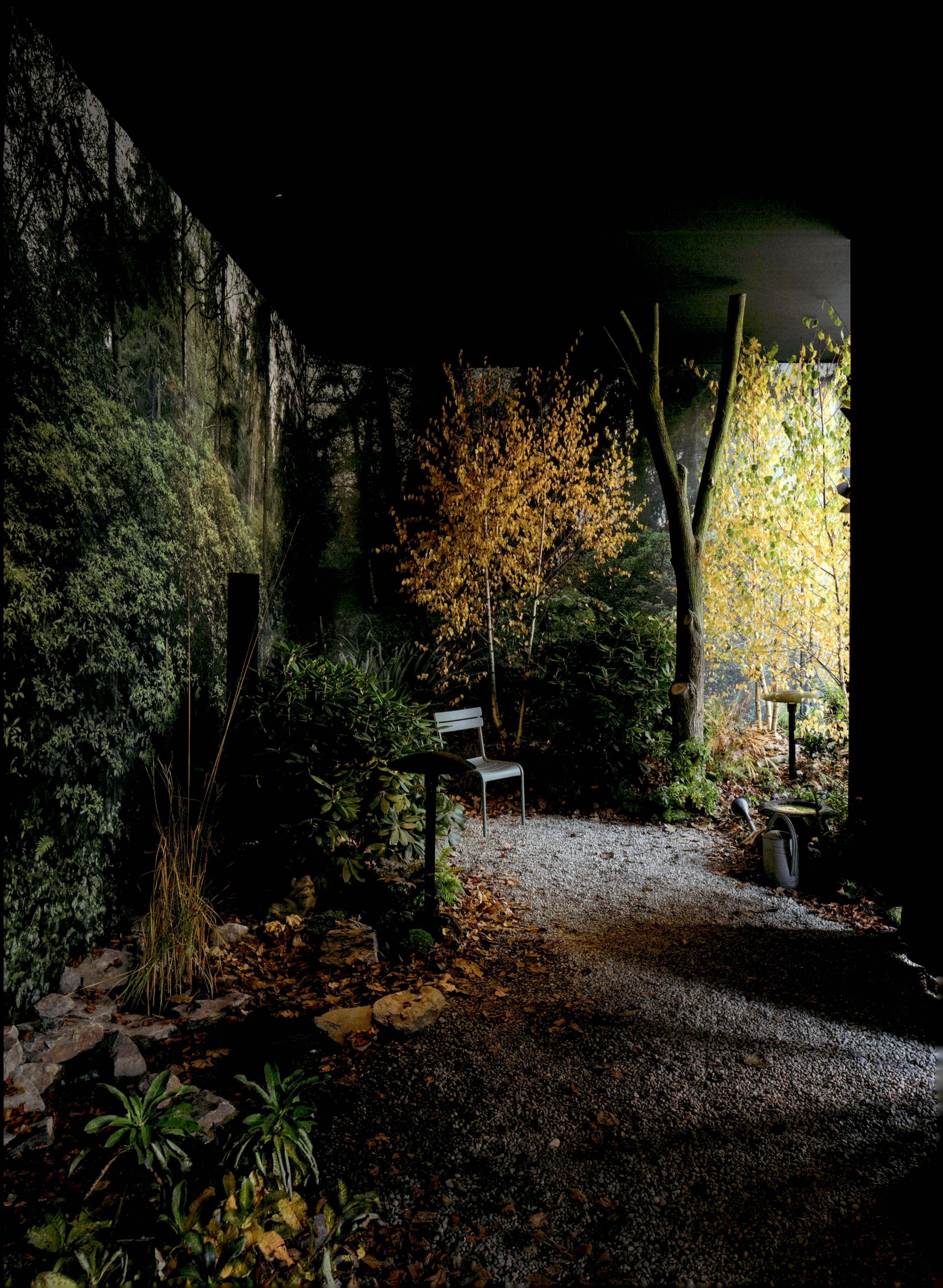

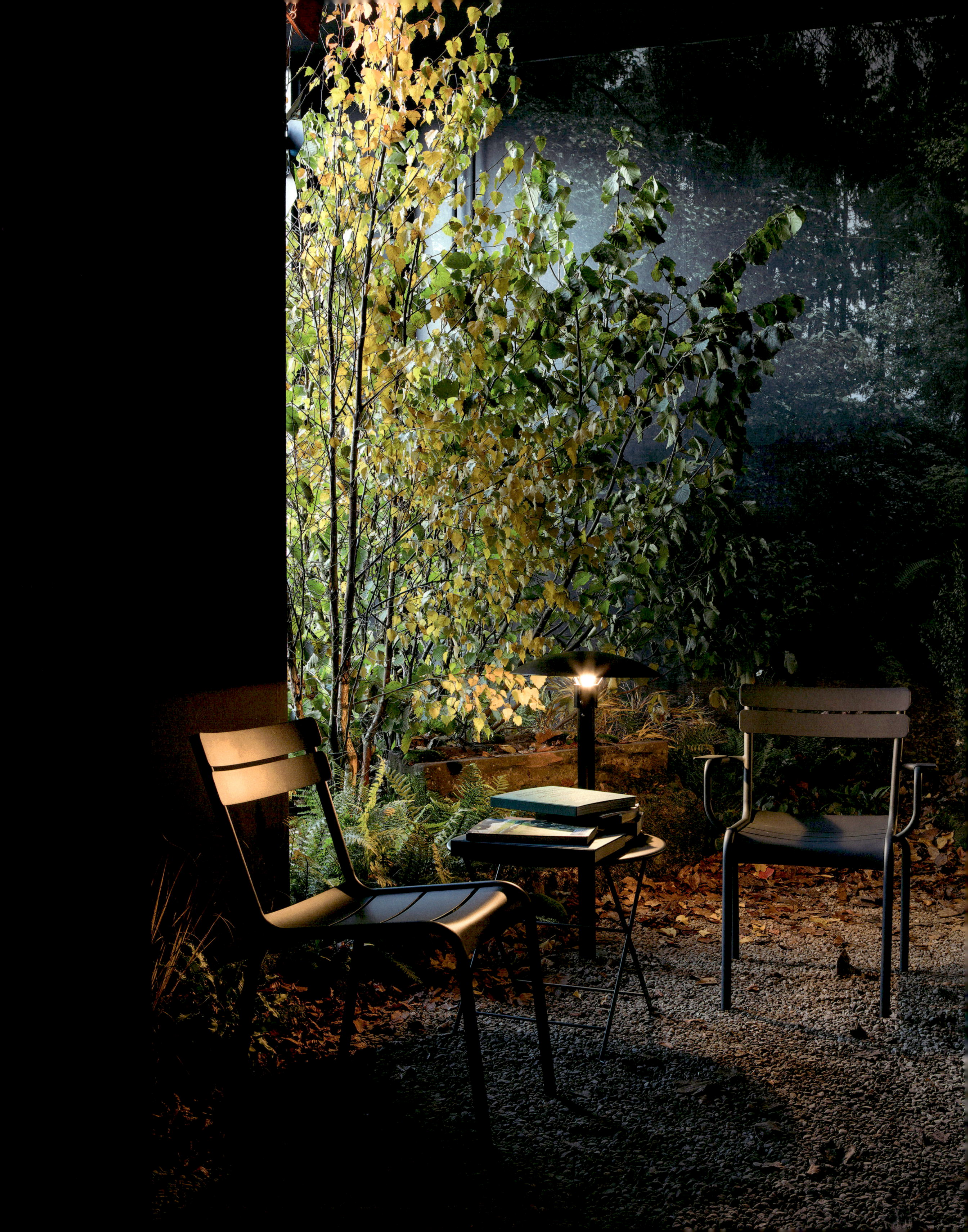

Martin Steinmann in conversation with Edelaar Mosayebi Inderbitzin

What distinguishes this exhibition is the fact that it is not based on plans and photographs but on the things themselves. We are confronted with the actual subject matter in question. We stand in a garden, but the garden has been planted in a room! This is a double alienation. On one hand, it is a real garden and not a picture of one; on the other, it is unreal, so it is a picture after all and not a garden, a kind of *tableau vivant*.

Martin Steinmann
We have tried to do justice to the place and have therefore taken a seat wearing our coats, for we are in a garden late in the year, as indicated by the dry leaves. But Ulrich Müller spoiled the impression by asking us take our coats off since we are indoors. By so doing he underscored the ambivalence of the exhibition: a garden, an outside space, installed inside.

Where are we – in a building or in a garden? And what is the exhibition about – architecture or nature? This touches on several of the issues we shall address in this conversation. In addition to the plants that we see when we look around the exhibition, there are the sounds, a bird calling, gravel crunching underfoot and the smell of the vegetation. Those are all imaginings related to the experience of architecture, and a means of arousing imaginings of our own.

The diorama, so very popular in the 19th century and known as *salle de miracle,* takes advantage of this twofold alienation. One of the first was built by Daguerre and described by Balzac as the miracle of the century. It burned down in 1839, the same year that Daguerre invented photography (Benjamin, *The Arcades Project,* p. 531).

A circular panorama in Lucerne depicts the surrender of Bourbaki's army in Switzerland in 1871, to similar effect. Painted by Edmond Castres and his assistants, it is 10 meters high and 112 meters long. The skill lies in arranging a variety of objects so that the transition from the painted to the real space occurs imperceptibly. It is not simply a matter of deception and illusion, but equally of the means through which we are deceived – and our delight in them.

MS Why did you use the device of a panorama for your exhibition at the Gallery of Architecture in Berlin?

Ron Edelaar
We wanted to generate an illusion. The staged garden was to resemble a real garden as closely as possible. On one hand, we wanted to do justice to Ulrich Müller's idea of not just exhibiting things in the room but of converting the room itself into the subject matter of the exhibition. On the other hand, the depth of detail required to generate that effect is directed against the abstraction, the smoothness and the one dimensionality of our reality. There's a kind of impish delight in this confrontation.

Beyond that, we were tantalized by the technical challenge of creating the effect we were aiming for. How do you create a mural so that the real planted space of the interior segues into the photographed space of the outdoors? What kind of lighting should you choose? What should the ceiling be like? In this respect, the making – the design and the construction – was easily as important as the outcome.

As far as the motif is concerned, we have long been interested in gardens. Elli and Christian had already written papers on the subject when they were still studying. From the very beginning, the garden has been a concern of ours in our work as architects. Broadly speaking, a garden refers to everything that is around a building; we are interested in the relationship between building and garden. In addressing this relationship we wanted a form that does not rely on pictures and plans. The room itself was to be the thing that the exhibition is about. Seen in this light, the exhibition is not complex.

In the folder for the exhibition, the architects write that the relationship between building and garden is crucial to their designs. On one level, that is a practical consideration: the relationship between inside and outside. This relationship is addressed in the exhibition – in reverse: when we stand outside and look through the window we do not see a room but a garden, another outside, which is an additional level and an answer to what the exhibition is about. I think the exhibition emphasises the relationship by alienating it or, in the words of Russian formalism, de-automatizing it. As a result, we are able to perceive the garden, and our relationship to gardens in general, with new eyes.

MS However, the installation is not restricted to creating a garden or the illusion of one. As I see it, it aims to make visitors think about the relationship between architecture and nature – specifically in terms of your work and the way in which you yourselves think about that relationship in the process of developing your designs. For you, it is a reciprocal relationship: the garden responds to the idea of the building; but the building, in turn, must also respond to the idea you have of its garden.

Christian Inderbitzin
True, in our designs we do intend to achieve a unity of building and garden, of inside and outside, so that they mutually condition and complement each other. With that in mind, we have tried out different strategies in our projects and developed different

themes. In the case of built space, the location naturally plays an important role in this relationship but we take an expanded view of context.

There is exciting potential in setting aside for the moment the real, spatial relationship of building and garden to investigate such things as applying the art of composing gardens to architectural design, in other words, exploring more abstract connections between architecture and landscape.

Elli Mosayebi
Whatever the case, that relationship has always been our point of departure. The cultural history of gardens and buildings is incredibly wide-ranging. It is our aim to study it and understand the wealth of implications. It's so fascinating to realise how fruitful such comparatively simple dichotomies can be: architecture and nature, building and garden, inside and outside, clean and dirty, wild and cultivated. The history of the relationship between gardens and buildings is a dense, far-reaching source of ever new ideas and inspiration.

On completing their studies at the ETH, Mosayebi and Inderbitzin wrote a detailed paper on the English Park in which they focused on the painterly aspect, the Picturesque. The paper is scientific even though its objective is to make the principles of the Picturesque fruitful to design. On writing it in 2008, the authors took a stand against the predilection for pure concept in Swiss architecture.

The Picturesque is a term that goes back to the seventeenth century, but it was not until the eighteenth century and nascent Romanticism that the notion acquired significance in both French painting and English gardens. Accordingly, the design of a garden is painting, just like the picture of a landscape hanging on the wall, as noted by the English poet and author Alexander Pope.

But this is not a seminar on the Picturesque or on gardening based on that concept. I am simply establishing a connection to an idea that contributes substantially to the architectural thinking of Edelaar Mosayebi Inderbitzin, namely, the mutual reciprocity of building and garden or of architecture and nature in general. The architects call it 'the idea of place'.

MS The design of a garden depends on the idea that you have of the place, on the way you perceive it. In that respect, you expand the notion of context. You do not restrict yourselves to identifying the features of a place. You also imagine the context, you speak of an 'imagined place', in other words, of the ideas that occur to you in connection with the real place.

CI That is indeed an important concept for us: the imagined context. The dominant issue when we studied at the ETH was the morphological and typological significance of context. Now, however, we are often confronted with places – in the periphery, for example – where a reading of the physical structures and forms has nothing to offer. It does not provide a reliable basis for design. So we expand the concept, trying to find ideas by way of association that we superimpose on the real place, as a kind of inner place. You might say, we try to infuse it architecturally and possibly even reveal its hidden essence. I think that's an important aspect of our work. It's something we discovered in the course of doing research on English culture.

MS One of your designs that I find particularly striking in its concentration is the Avellana housing project in Zurich-Schwamendingen. You saw the place as fallow land, without form or shape, and incorporated that idea into the design of the garden, so that it now resembles ruderal land. It matches the design of the building, which is somehow similarly spontaneous in appearance.

CI As mentioned, something begins to attract our attention when we take a more abstract turn. One feature of gardens, even designed gardens, is the considerable degree of openness, of formlessness. The appearance of the natural world is related to growth and decay; it is subject to constant change. Aiming for this openness of form can be very appealing in architecture as well.

Regarding the project that you mentioned, it's situated at the edge of a former village, with gardens and spontaneously built sheds. This situation interested us and is mirrored in the design: in the composition of the volume, in the positioning of the windows, and also in the way the apartments are accessed. You walk directly into the kitchen, as one used to in farmhouses. This stands in contrast to the urban, bourgeois layout of apartments, which is alien to this location.

The English garden was a composition of landscape and built elements that were meant to look picturesque, in other words, 'natural'. The garden was not a matter of nature but of culture, its natural countenance was created artificially, its composition governed by specific ideas. This applies, in its own way, to the housing project in Schwamendingen. Small willows were planted to appear as if they had grown spontaneously. In this case, the idea of naturalness plays a role by taking the shape of unused land left to itself. The idea also underpins the spontaneous, formless qualities of the architecture.

That means that the structural features are not givens; instead they have been assigned to the place. An essay that I wrote about another housing project by these architects is titled 'The Place as Idea'. Their approach might be described as retroactive contextualism. You acquire an idea of a place that springs from a diversity of images and memories and then design a building that projects this idea onto the place. Accordingly, in their folder for the exhibition, the architects write that gardens are as fascinating for being conceived spaces as they are for being constructed spaces, in other words, that they can be experienced both in the mind and through the body.

EM The housing project in Schwamendingen is meant to look as if it had grown spontaneously, bit by bit, like sheds that are constantly modified. That objective is contradictory by definition. How can planning produce spontaneous, accidental results?

We came across a means of tackling this question while preparing for our trip to England. In his book *Sweet Disorder and the Carefully Careless* (1997), Robert Maxwell describes the design method that cultivates the accidental, the informal and the casual. That was our challenge as well: How can you make a built object look as if it had been 'unplanned'? That was a different approach to design from what we had learned at the ETH, where all decisions had to be pulled from finished, self-contained concepts. Extremely self-referential concepts of that kind characterise Swiss architecture of the 1990s. We wanted something different for our Avellana housing project.

CI The project is a deliberately artificial composition but it leads to openness, which is important because the tenants perceive its appearance in different ways. We have to assume a plurality of interpretations. The 'open form' can elicit heterogeneous individual impressions. Let's take the colours: there are four shades of green. They could be different but they define a space. The idea of colour as such was therefore more important than the specific choice of colour.

In other projects, for example the project in Zurich-Hottingen, the idea of an open form is present elsewhere. The ground plans kept changing in the process of the work. The way they were finally built represents a 'possible form'. They could be different; the metamorphoses – in the sense of Ovid – could have continued. You might say that we build possible forms. But that doesn't mean that they are imprecise or arbitrary. The openness that they generate is intrinsic to the design.

RE There are also considerable practical advantages: The open form that we devise is robust. When clients propose wishes of one kind or another, the open form may well be able to accommodate them without weakening the building as a whole.

The last time I visited the studio of Edelaar Mosayebi Inderbitzin, one of the walls was covered with photographs of gardens, untold varieties of gardens, obviously source material for a competition that they were working on. I think the wall illustrates a procedure that younger architects call 'referencing'. It consists of studying pictures from different places and times to work out an 'idea of place' that gradually takes concrete shape in the process of designing. It is not a linear procedure; the pictures lead to decisions, the decisions in turn lead to other pictures.

This is not new in itself but for me it was new to note that they are all equivalent, in other words, all equally suitable as references without some of them being ruled out as 'foreign'. One might speak of cultural globalisation. What the subject matters of the photographs mean and meant within their respective culture seems to be of no relevance. They are now generally accessible materials for design regardless of those meanings. The experiences of which they are the result do not count; what counts are the experiences that might be constructed by using them. The design process incorporates those other meanings in the sense of multiple coding.

MS As I understand it, working with pictures as references does not involve critical investigation. It is not about *critica operativa,* as it was called in the 1970s – in other words, inquiry into architectural codes by working with them. So, it is basically only a matter of acquiring sources for the design process.

CI Yes, we work with references and we have a clear idea of how we go about it. The background for that is the ETH, or more precisely, Analogue Architecture. But we take a different approach. We are not interested in the formal aspect of references as 'pictures' but rather in their structural features and the underlying ideas that we glean from them. We try to understand those features and make productive use of them in the course of the design process.

The Hottingen project illustrates that. We studied countless natural forms, especially rock formations, like basalt. We were fascinated to note the almost architectural expression of such formations. We studied their structure and their features in reference to the volumetric composition of the building. The vertical, pilaster-like wall sections relate to the mighty tree trunks nearby. So working with references does not mean 're-constructing' them, but rather discovering and working with their structural features.

RE Our main interest in the pictures you saw on the wall of our studio was not the gardens depicted in them; we studied them to find ideas for a ground plan. A lot of the pictures we draw on as references do not show architecture but come from the fine arts or other disciplines. Machines often come into play as well.

MS So it's not the meaning of the things, the pictures, but rather their structure that is important in these references. That makes me wonder what criteria guide your choice.

EM Naturally, we try to define and justify the choice objectively. But I do believe that it starts out with being fascinated by a picture. Initially we just choose pictures subjectively and intuitively. Something strikes us as beautiful, as a specific expression of something and we want to know why.

CI … a subjective selection, yes, but it's ultimately about the underlying idea. You spoke about cultural globalisation. To my mind, the world of ideas has always been global, ideas have always migrated. Think of the naïve classicism in the North that shows how fascinated people were by the South.

MS You are quite right, of course. There was knowledge, early on, of what was going on in other regions of the world. Chinese gardens, for instance, were known and re-created in Europe in the 18th century, including their pavilions. I'm thinking of the Chinese House, built in 1764 in the park of Sanssouci after sketches by Frederick the Great. But those were Chinoiseries.

There is something else that concerns me about the current use of references. Pictures fascinated us in the 1970s, too, and we tried to understand their underlying ideas. I may be biased but I don't see this kind of inquiry in today's so-called referencing. The pictures are treated as pictures, without exploring the 'reason for the form'. That's why machines can also be references. I don't criticize that but I wonder what it's about.

EM A picture exerts a fascination and, as mentioned, one wants to know why. But maybe we look for answers not so much in the pictures themselves but rather in the way they potentially relate to a project. The project integrates them so that something singular and new emerges. The singularity is the reason for the form. We are not doing research in order to find a reason for using certain references in a project.

CI Nor do we want references to be 'visible' in the final project. That's why we talk about understanding them structurally so that they influence the design on an abstract level. That's what distinguishes them from Analogue Architecture, where the imagery is often still recognisable.

MS Even when you talk about understanding things structurally, I think – regarding the references – it's more about the effect of a form, than about material conditions, it's about what Adolf Loos called 'the reason of form'. That is demonstrated by the term Picturesque. It's a procedure that makes it possible to associate different things.

CI Exactly! That's what fascinates us about the parks and gardens in England. An extremely natural approach to landscape design is combined with neo-Palladian architecture. Very different things are united through deliberate composition and, in the end, they yield a 'picture'. Such ends are not only achieved by the Picturesque; one might also speak of collage, for example.

MS But in contrast to collage, the pieces of a picturesque composition can no longer be distinguished. They have basically fused into a whole.

CI It works both ways presumably. The villa in the above example is still 'classical' and the landscape is still 'natural'. Formally they remain autonomous, but they enter into a relationship that can no longer be dissolved.

The imagery that comes into play is material for a design that creates moods. I thus name a venerable term in the history of gardens, which is related to the Picturesque. Christian Cay Laurenz Hirschfeld has much to say about that in his *Theorie der Gartenkunst* (1775). It is not enough for a garden artist to have extensive knowledge of various landscapes, for, as Hirschfeld writes, he must also be familiar with all the effects of these on the human spirit for that is the true study of nature (Hirschfeld, p. 55). Garden art does not affect us through a remote imitation but instantly grips our senses, striking directly at our emotions through the presence of actual objects, without filtering them through memory and imagination (Hirschfeld, p. 57–58).

Hirschfeld distinguishes gardens according to their mood: the cheerful garden, the melancholy garden ... And he specifies the means of creating such effects: plants, water, even birds. Anyone who has meandered through the two gardens in Sanssouci that Peter Joseph Lenné laid out in 1857–1860, has experienced both the different moods and the means of creating them: cheerful, the so-called Sicilian Garden; grave, with its dark conifers, the Nordic Garden. Hirschfeld would call it melancholic, where isolation, darkness and stillness must reign in all parts and must prove their powerful effect on the soul (Hirschfeld, p. 165). In this respect, the picturesque garden of the 18th century signified a liberation from the styles that could not be enjoyed without knowledge of their underlying codes.

Garden art therefore assists in creating a mood that reveals the 'idea of a place'. In the housing project in Schwamendingen and the memories it evokes, the design of the surroundings creates a mood of the provisional, unplanned and formless that the architects found to be characteristic of the location. Architecture and nature are a mutual reinforcement in constructing that mood.

MS Your invitation to have a conversation about gardens made me think of Hirschfeld's book. Some of his sentences could be yours. It is his aim to understand a place and then create a design that will enhance its effect: its effect on the human spirit, as he says more than once. He writes about the mood that can be generated by a garden – or indeed by any space. Mood was a much debated concern of the late 18th century. Does it mean anything to you? Are the pictures that you use in arriving at your designs related to the effect that can be created by a mood? Do they have anything to do with you?

CI Elsewhere, we have mentioned that we find the term 'mood' challenging to deal with. It is not an architectural term, though there is no denying that it has an effect. Every space creates a certain mood. But I don't think that we design with a view to implementing a specific mood.

RE To return to working the notion of references: pictures, that is references, that occur to us as we design are often related to experiences of some kind: we travel, we see things, we see them in a certain mood, and we remember them. You said that mood describes a spiritual effect and that it is individual. We do not design a mood; we design spaces that might generate a mood, for example, spaces that are darker than others. Tensions create moods and that's what interests us.

EM There's always an atmosphere, or a mood. We're fully aware of that. And of course we do think about what kind of atmosphere we want to generate: should a space feel open or cheerful? For the Guggach housing project, we asked ourselves: How do we create an urban atmosphere outdoors at the edge of a forest?

So we address the question of atmosphere from the very beginning. It doesn't come afterwards; it's incorporated in the choice of references. We don't use the term very often but it is part of the narrative, part of our approach to design. It plays a big role and derives from references and our own experiences. We test what we want to do on the basis of our own experiences. So atmosphere is certainly part of the design process.

Two terms occur with regularity on listening to Edelaar Mosayebi Inderbitzin: the Picturesque and the open form. They both feature in two research projects conducted by Mosayebi and Inderbitzin after completing their studies at the ETH (*Bomarzo. Beobachtungen anhand einer Karte*, 2005 and *The Picturesque – Synthese im Bildhaften*, 2008). In outlining the design process cultivated in their work, they speak, in their essay 'Modell und Bild', about two overlapping terms. They describe the open form as potentially multi-layered, multipartite, impure, indistinct and therefore ambivalent. These features leave the open form semantically undefined. Such features are also characteristic of nature, whose forms are subject to constant change.

The other term is the Picturesque or the picturesque form, which they use to refer to a synthetic, though 'soft', means of establishing an order. Characteristic of both terms are the blurred edges of their features. They treat the Picturesque as a kind of cement that links the impure and semantically undefined with the pure and the classical, with the self-evident, dialectically open-ended approach. This they call the 'synthetic' power of the Picturesque. The connection takes the shape of a picture. The picture constitutes a whole in which the combined constituents acquire new meaning. In English gardens, architectural and natural elements are combined to form a 'landscape', a term that turns the perception of diverse elements into a whole.

MS When you apply several references to one project, you give viewers room for interpretation.

CI That's an aspect we've already touched on and it's important to us: the open form. It eludes clear-cut definition; it is semantically open-ended. Our study of the Picturesque laid the foundations for that approach. Texts, like Umberto Eco's *The Open Work*, subsequently led to our terminology. According to Eco, a modern work of art is open to various interpretations.

MS And, as he writes elsewhere, it's the readers who tell its story, who make it real, as it were, on the basis of their own experiences. These suffice to appreciate the work of art.

EM You use the word 'story'. We use the term 'narrative'. It is an important aspect of design. After becoming familiar with all the conditions of an assignment, one has to find a point of departure. In a competition that we are currently involved in, it's the client's passion for gardens. That's a good starting point for developing a narrative, which requires research and then implementation. That characterises all of our projects, they all have a narrative. When I listen to the way we are talking about our projects here, I realise that we really are telling stories. We develop them during the design process and write them down when we submit our competition entry. They not only explain our projects; they are, in fact, their substance.

MS To me that seems to be a contradiction: on one hand, narratives guide your designs, and yet you aspire to a form that has access to several interpretations, in other words, several narratives. Aren't your narratives more than a substance that causes a chemical reaction in the process of design and is released again at the end? Or do I have to be aware of them in order to understand the projects?

CI No, that would indeed contradict the open form. Perhaps the language of narrative, as we understand it, is like a kind of dream language: there is a plot, a story in dreams, but it always breaks off and goes somewhere else. Bits and pieces are comprehensible but on the whole, dreams can be extremely open and can point in different directions.

We find architecture boring when it focuses exclusively on material and has a form that purports to mean nothing. We seek to strike a balance between forms that mean something and are understood as such, and forms whose effect is more 'abstract', relying, for example, largely on the sensual effect of a material. And we're always having to find a new balance, which is what makes each of the projects look so different.

EM Instead of specifying concepts and working from there, we start with a much more tenuous structure. The narrative describes the design process and not the story as a self-contained whole. We tell one another stories when we're designing – stories about the place, about the architectural shape and about the activities of the future tenants. At some point they come together; at some point the project stands alone. Certain aspects of the stories are palpable; others are read into the project. As authors, we write the stories but we can't govern how the building will be perceived. But we do believe that this design approach produces projects that give users much more leeway for interpretation.

In the introduction to their paper on the Picturesque, the authors explain that their research is motivated by the fact that numerous contemporary designs blur the boundaries between architecture and nature. They are interested in exploring at what point architecture merges with the natural and in finding out where tectonic structures border on the Picturesque. Ultimately, they are motivated by the venerable wish to reconcile culture and nature, which, as they say, may be fulfilled, possibly for the first time ever, in our post-agrarian age (Mosayebi, Inderbitzin, p. 13). To them, the burgeoning field of landscape architecture is an indication of that reconciliation.

This suggests two questions, a theoretical one and a practical one. The first reads: Does reconciliation mean that building and garden condition each other as *pars pro toto,* that a design is necessarily the combination of both, that 'a building today is only interesting if it is more than itself' (Smithson, *Without Rhetoric: An Architectural Aesthetic 1955–1972*, p. 36)? Of course, that applies to any context and any means of garnering criteria for design and also to the relationship of the two disciplines in the design process. That takes us to the second question: How do architect and landscape architect actually work together?

MS Does the garden start out as an 'idea of place', which you develop and which is later carried out by the landscape architect, or does it emerge in mutual dependence on the two disciplines? And in the latter case, how do architect and landscape architect work together?

RE When working on a design, it is fruitful for the discourse on architecture to go beyond individual disciplines. Our exhibition would not have been designed so well without Daniel Ganz. The exchange with him and other landscape architects during the design process was invaluable. In other cases, however, the landscape architect is called in only to implement a specified design.

EM We spoke about the idea of an imagined place. In many cases, the place itself does not suffice to give architecture a concrete identity. Let's take the large estate in Guggach: the land is located between woods on one side and a large street on the other. What do you do with the courtyard that is bracketed by the buildings? We soon realised that it must be clearly distinguished from the woods and must assimilate artificial, urban properties in this clearly urban location. So we introduced large flat basins of water that resonate with the cast glass surfaces of the façades. Like the façades, the basins reflect the changing light and they form a whole in combination with the buildings. The project would have less impact without these basins.

CI The surface of the water transforms the courtyard into a distinctive space and radically changes the way the buildings relate to the ground. We looked at the outdoor spaces of the estates built by Fernand Pouillon in Paris; they are very architectural. The surroundings in Guggach have a lot to do with the French notion of designed nature.

The maintenance of the basins – over one thousand square meters in size – requires a great deal of equipment, which is accommodated in the cellar. Here nature consists only of a kind of 'skin'; the topmost layer is nature, but underneath there is a machine. That seems very French to us, comparable to the fountains in Versailles: they can't operate without technology either.

MS The artificiality is obvious but that applies to all projects, even in eighteenth-century England. Picturesque parks were staged by using natural means.

CI Even Capability Brown had tons of earth shifted about in order to create an impression of nature.

There is another link between architecture and nature, a kind of 'inner' relationship. The provisional atmosphere of the Schwamendingen project is not restricted to its outside appearance; it also influences the loose arrangement of the rooms inside. In other words, there is a rapport between the experience of architecture and of nature, the one reinforces the other. The housing that Edelaar Mosayebi Inderbitzin built in an old garden in Hottingen is a striking example of this rapport. Circulation through the flats resembles a meandering garden path that offers surprising views of the 'landscape' in the spirit of the Picturesque. And because the path meanders, the flats seem larger, as in Hirschfeld's description of smaller gardens, in which meandering paths can also serve to excite an appearance of enlargement (Hirschfeld, p. 141).

The image of a path evokes another aspect of the rapport between architecture and nature regarding movement through a building. Movement has always been part of architectural thinking in various forms, for instance, functional movement in the spirit of

Taylorism, movement as a social act or the aimless movement of an architectural promenade. In many examples of more recent architecture, this latter type of movement deviates from Le Corbusier's intent, for it is more picturesque, closer to the model of the Picturesque: circulating through the flats in Hottingen is like walking through an English park, the path turns this way and that, becomes wide and narrow, light and dark ... What's crucial is the sensual experience and the fact that it is an experience unto itself, like taking a walk, as demonstrated by Edelaar Mosayebi Inderbitzin's Hottingen project.

Ulrich Müller
The exhibition is titled *Garden*. We never talked about what kind of a garden it would be. Garden is a completely open-ended term. But: is it a garden? There are plants that don't actually appear in gardens. A number of visitors said to me that maybe it was once a landscaped garden, now given over to the rampant growth of nature.

CI It is a fern garden. We are familiar with gardens of that kind and used ferns intentionally. But that's not the point. You are talking about an overgrown garden, the garden as a ruin. That is a very important image for us, or rather an important metaphor – and on several levels. A ruin is a hybrid between architecture and nature. In that respect, it symbolises our idea of an open form because it takes the form of transmuting into formlessness. But maybe it also stands for an image of the world. In our world, in our cities, we are confronted with fragments, fractions, torsos. So could one say that the world resembles a ruin? It is a term that we have come across in our work with gardens and it helps us as a mental construct.

UM You laid out books from your library on a table in the garden, among them, a picture book about ruins.

CI *Zauber der Vergänglichkeit* (Pleasure of Ruins) by Macaulay and Beny.

UM The notion of a ruin resonates in the architectural fragments that you incorporated in the exhibition. They are vehicles of meaning; as fragments they tell stories. As I recall, we also talked about the concept of Romanticism when we were preparing the exhibition. A ruin can be interpreted in different ways but it is clearly a romantic image. There's an entry in the guestbook: I would like to spend the night here. For many visitors, the exhibition was like a place of longing.

CI We don't want to contradict that. But we are not interested so much in the Romanticism, that is, the romantic aspect of ruins, as we are in their structural features. Ruins were already important in the Renaissance; they are not a phenomenon that is confined to Romanticism. They have always had meaning, but different meanings.

RE We don't think romantically, but we feel that way.

Literature

Martin Steinmann: 'Der Ort als Idee', in: *werk, bauen + wohnen,* 6–2016, pp. 24–31.

Christian Inderbitzin: 'Modell und Bild', in: *trans 19,* ETH Zurich 2011, pp. 86–91.

Elli Mosayebi and Christian Inderbitzin: *The Picturesque – Synthese im Bildhaften,* Zurich: gta Verlag, 2008.

Adrian Searle, Kitty Scott and Catherine Grenier: *Peter Doig,* London/New York: Phaidon Press, 2007.

Elli Mosayebi and Christian Inderbitzin: *Bomarzo. Beobachtungen anhand einer neuen Karte,* Zurich: gta Verlag, 2005.

Aleida Assmann, Monika Gomille and Gabriele Rippl (ed.): *Ruinenbilder,* Paderborn: Wilhelm Fink, 2002.

Robert Maxwell: *Sweet Disorder and the Carefully Careless: Theory and Criticism in Architecture,* New York: Princeton Architectural Press, 1993.

Walter Benjamin: *Das Passagen-Werk,* Vol. 2, Berlin: Suhrkamp, 1983.

Adrian von Buttlar: *Der englische Landsitz 1715–1760. Symbol eines liberalen Weltentwurfs,* Falkenberg: Mäander, 1982.

Siegmar Gerndt: *Idealisierte Natur. Die literarische Kontroverse um den Landschaftsgarten des 18. und frühen 19. Jahrhunderts in Deutschland,* Stuttgart: J. B. Metzler, 1981.

Umberto Eco: *Das offene Kunstwerk,* Berlin: Suhrkamp, 1977.

Alison and Peter Smithson: *Without Rhetoric: An Architectural Aesthetic 1955–1972,* Cambridge, Massachusetts: M.I.T. Press, 1974.

Rose Macaulay and Roloff Beny: *Zauber der Vergänglichkeit,* Munich/Zurich: Droemer Knaur, 1966.

M. H. Baillie Scott: *Houses and Gardens,* London: G. Newnes, 1906.

Horace Walpole: 'On Modern Gardening', in: Horace Walpole (ed.), *Anecdotes of Painting in England,* Vol. 3, London: H. G. Bohn, 1862.

Christian Cay Laurenz Hirschfeld: *Theorie der Gartenkunst,* Leipzig: Weidmann u. Reich, 1775.

Biographies

Stephen Bates

Stephen Bates (*1964) is a founding partner of Sergison Bates architects. Established in 1996, the practice was awarded the Heinrich Tessenow Gold Medal and the Erich Schelling Medal for Architecture in 2006. Many of their projects have received awards and their work has been exhibited at a number of international venues, including the Venice Architecture Biennale in 2008 and 2012. Together with Jonathan Sergison, Stephen Bates has taught at a number of schools of architecture, including the Architectural Association in London, ETH Zurich, EPF Lausanne, the Oslo School of Architecture and the Harvard Graduate School of Design. He is currently Professor of Urbanism and Housing at TU München. Through the development of numerous projects in practice and his teaching role, he has explored the practical and theoretical aspects of city-making and domesticity and written extensively on issues raised by the relationship between the two different scales.

Daniel Ganz

Daniel Ganz (*1961) founded the Zurich-based office Ganz Landschaftsarchitekten in 1995, whose projects include the landscape architecture of the renovated ETH Polyterasse, the garden of C.G. Jung's house in Küsnacht and the gardens of Terminal E at Zurich Airport. Originally trained as a gardener, he studied landscape architecture under Dieter Kienast in Rapperswil, afterwards working for several years in Kingston, Jamaica. Alongside his practice he regularly lectures and has previously held teaching positions as Guest Professor at the EPF Lausanne 2011/2012 and at the Hochschule für Technik in Rapperswil 2008–2012. He joined Studio Tom Emerson at ETH Zurich in 2015.

Martin Steinmann

Martin Steinmann (*1942) completed his studies in architecture at the ETH Zurich in 1967. He worked as an architect in the office of Ernst Gisel, as assistant to Prof. Adolf Max Vogt and was on the staff of the Institute for the History and Theory of Architecture GTA. He completed his doctoral thesis on the Congrès Internationaux d'Architecture Moderne CIAM in 1978. In 1979, he was a Visiting Professor at MIT and taught at various schools of architecture, including the ETH Zurich. From 1980 to 1986 he was the editor of the magazine *archithese* in Zurich, and from 1987 to 2006 Professor of Architecture and Architectural Theory at the EPF Lausanne. He currently lives and works in Aarau. Steinmann has published widely on the architecture of the 20th and 21st centuries. In 2016, he was awarded the Grand Prix Suisse d'Art.

Edelaar Mosayebi Inderbitzin Architekten

Ron Edelaar (*1976), Elli Mosayebi (*1977), and Christian Inderbitzin (*1977) founded their architectural firm in Zurich in 2005. The firm's broad scope of work encompasses building projects – from design to construction – and urban planning along with exhibitions and publications. Housing represents a main focus of their research, teaching, and practice. Since 2011, major projects have been realized through routine collaboration with Baumberger & Stegmeier Architekten. Elli Mosayebi has been Professor for Design and Housing at TU Darmstadt since 2012. Christian Inderbitzin taught at the EPF Lausanne in 2015/2016. Ron Edelaar, Elli Mosayebi and Christian Inderbitzin were enrolled as members of the Federation of Swiss Architects in 2014. In 2017/2018 Edelaar Mosayebi Inderbitzin are teaching at ETH Zurich. www.emi-architekten.ch

Acknowledgements

We wish to express our cordial thanks to all those, including institutions and businesses, who stood by us and generously supported our exhibition and this publication. To begin with, we wish to thank Ulrich Müller for inviting us to mount an exhibition at the Architektur Galerie Berlin and for the constructive conversations with him in the process of planning the exhibition and carrying it out. Our special gratitude goes to Daniel Ganz for his intense collaboration in Zurich and on site in Berlin – without him we could not have mounted the exhibition in this form. We thank Stephen Bates and Martin Steinmann for their warm-hearted introduction and the inspiring conversation. Their enriching complement to the exhibition has now become an important part of this publication. We are indebted to photographer Markus Bühler-Rasom for his spontaneous and professional expertise in taking pictures of Seleger Moor for the mural. We thank Paradiesfabrik GmbH, Floressenz and Filmbauarbeiter GmbH in Berlin for their careful, committed and helpful contribution to the production. And what would we do without the unstinting commitment of our staff: Theres Hollenstein, Andrea Grolimund, Katharina Sommer, Lukas Burkhart, Simon Cheung, Jenna Buttermann and Charlotte Nobre. Finally, we thank Valentin Hindermann and Maike Hamacher of Büro 146 for the design of the publication, Catherine Schelbert and Louise Stein for the translation and critical reading of the texts and Thomas Kramer of Park Books for his speedy agreement to publish the book, his organizational support and his faith in our project.

Exhibition sponsors and supporters

Support of public organisations: Pro Helvetia, Swiss Arts Council; Main sponsors: Baugenossenschaft Glattal Zürich, Careal Immobilien AG, Müller Forch GmbH, Ralbau AG; Sponsors: ASTOR Küchen AG, Bächli Tiefbau GmbH, Baugenossenschaft Süd-Ost, Collofunda AG, Deutsche Steinzeug Schweiz AG, Dr. Lüchinger + Meyer Bauingenieure AG, Durlum AG, Erbengemeinschaft Kälin, Eternit Schweiz AG, Familie Nüscheler, Familie Steiger, Fenster Nauer AG, Lauber Iwisa, Mooris AG, Motorsänger GmbH, Park Seleger Moor, Planungsbüro Roman Böni GmbH, Postfinance AG, Preisig AG, Signau House Zürich AG, Stieger Bauten AG, STW AG für Raumplanung, Tulux AG, Vesely Fassadenagentur, Windler Innenausbau AG, WKP Bauingenieure AG, wlw Bauingenieure AG, Wohnbaugenossenschaft Bahoge.

The exhibition *Garden* was on view at the Architektur Galerie Berlin from 3 November to 17 December 2016. The conversation with Edelaar Mosayebi Inderbitzin Architekten and Martin Steinmann took place on 15 December 2016.

Imprint

Book concept and editing:
Edelaar Mosayebi Inderbitzin Architekten
Translations: Catherine Schelbert
Copy editing and proofreading: Louise Stein
Design: Büro 146. Maike Hamacher, Valentin Hindermann, Madeleine Stahel, Zurich
Lithography and Printing: Druckerei Odermatt AG, Dallenwil
Binding: BUBU AG, Mönchaltorf

List of Illustrations

p. 8–20: Roland Bernath, Zurich
p. 6, 29–40: Jan Bitter, Berlin
Book cover, p. 1, 2, 63–68: Edelaar Mosayebi Inderbitzin Architekten

Park Books
Niederdorfstrasse 54
8001 Zurich
Switzerland
www.park-books.com

Park Books is being supported by the Federal Office of Culture with a general subsidy for the years 2016–2020.

ISBN 978-3-03860-079-4

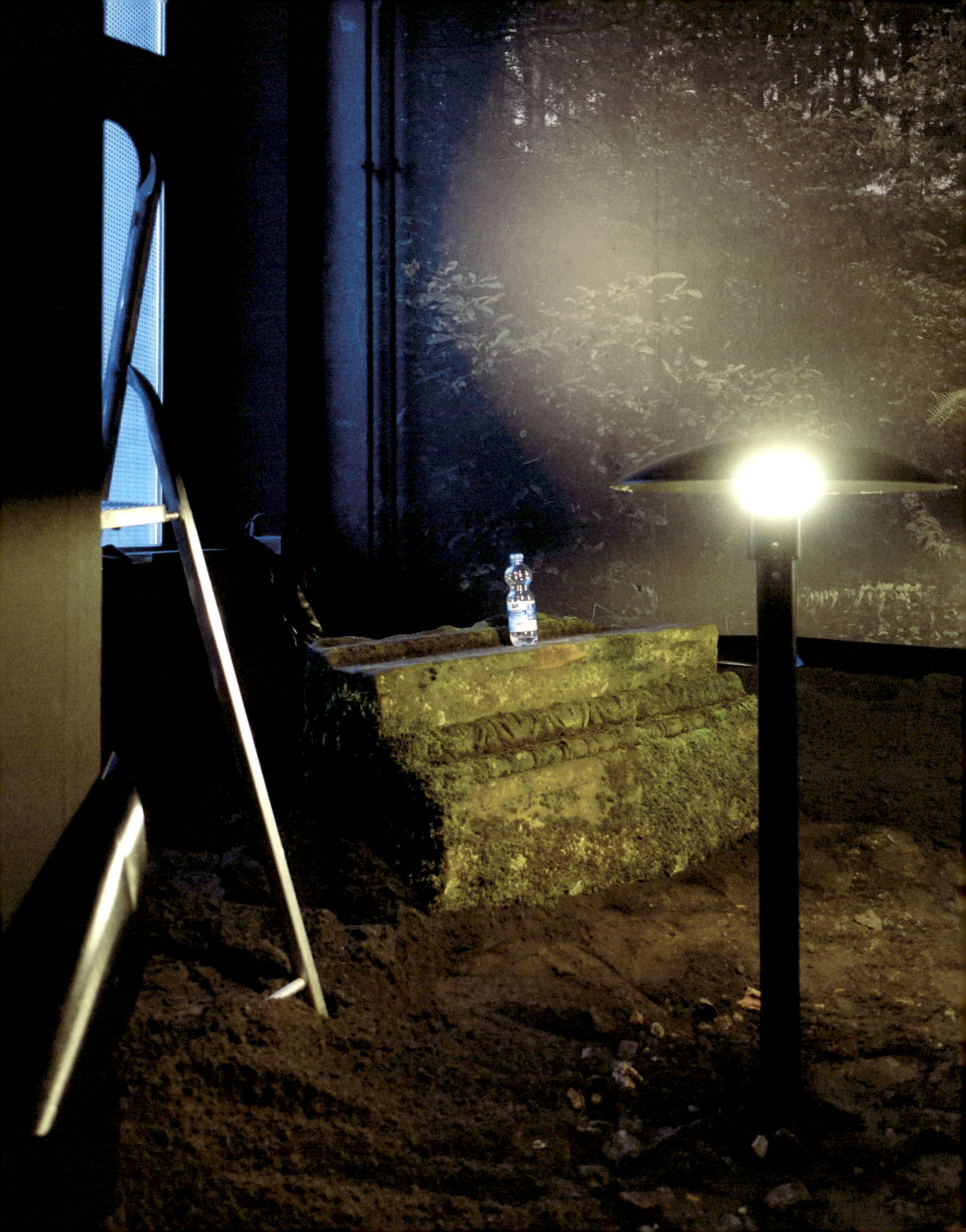

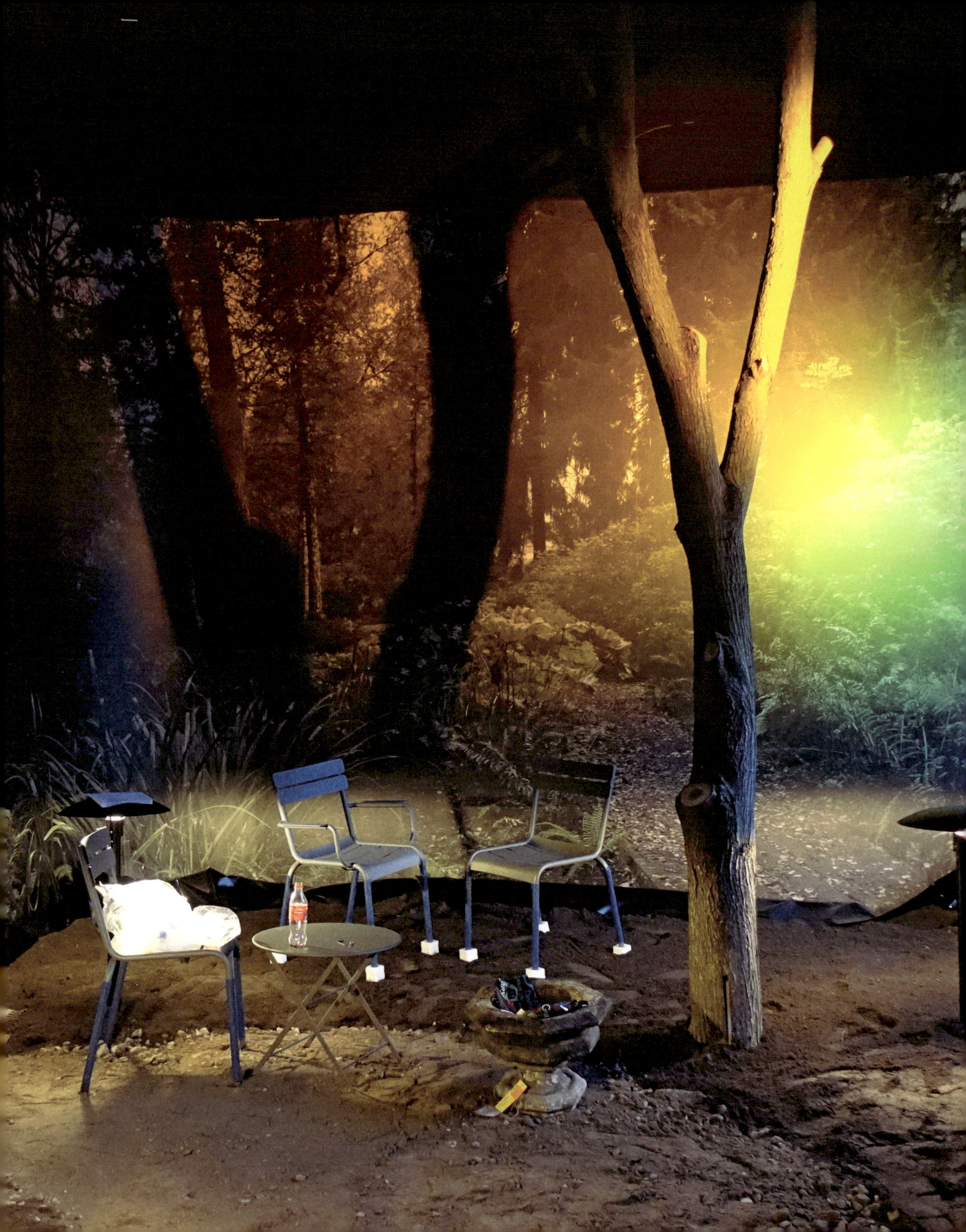

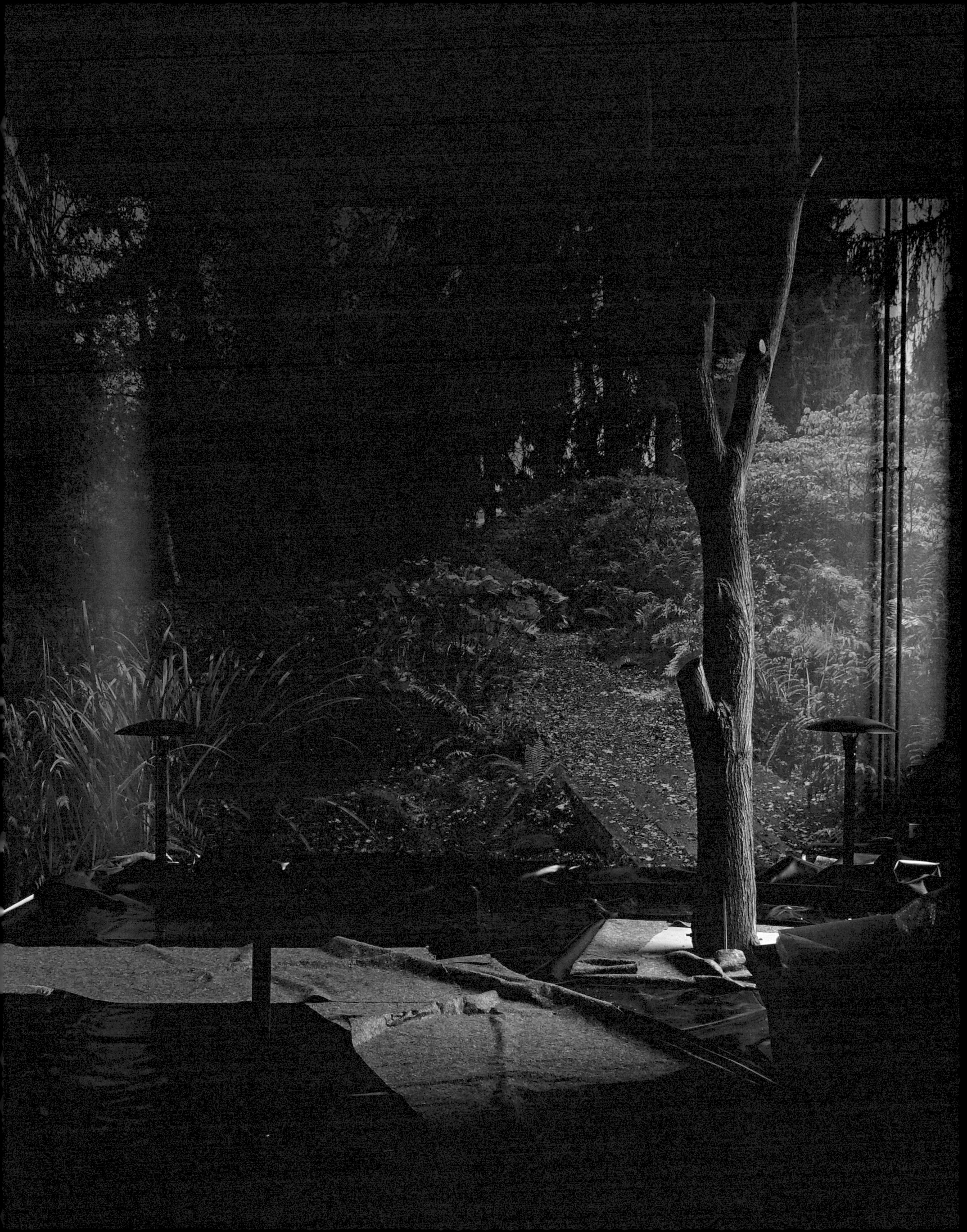

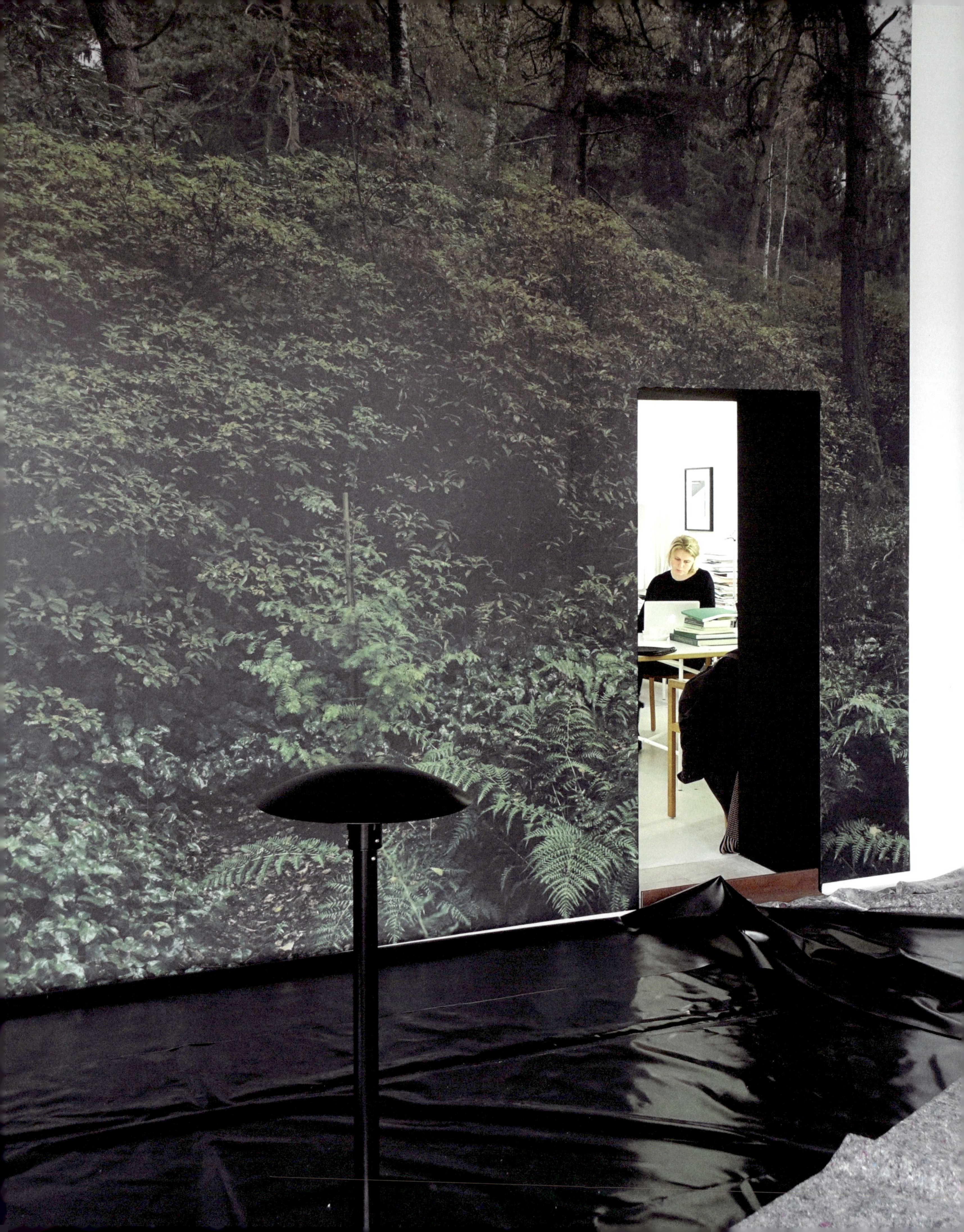

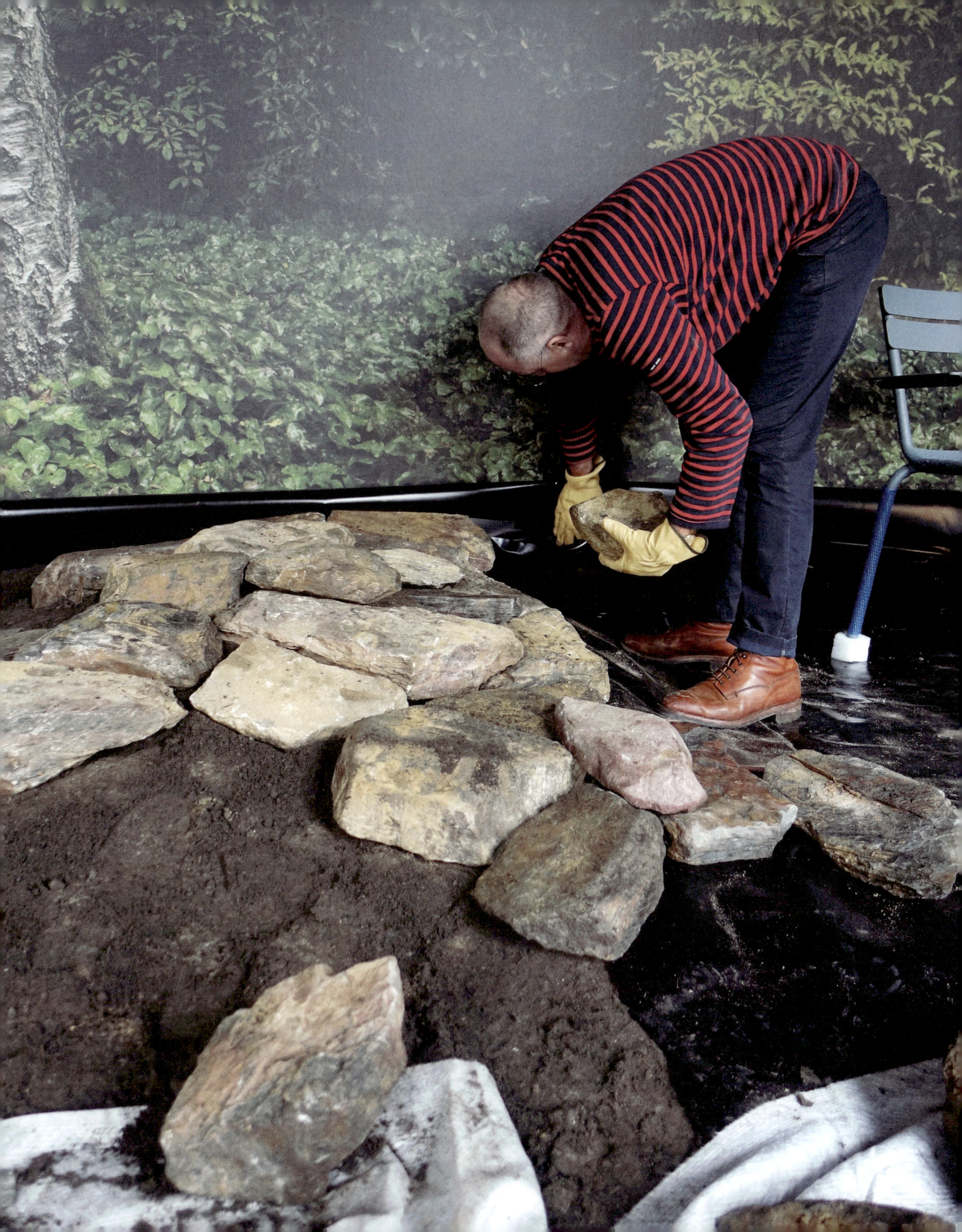

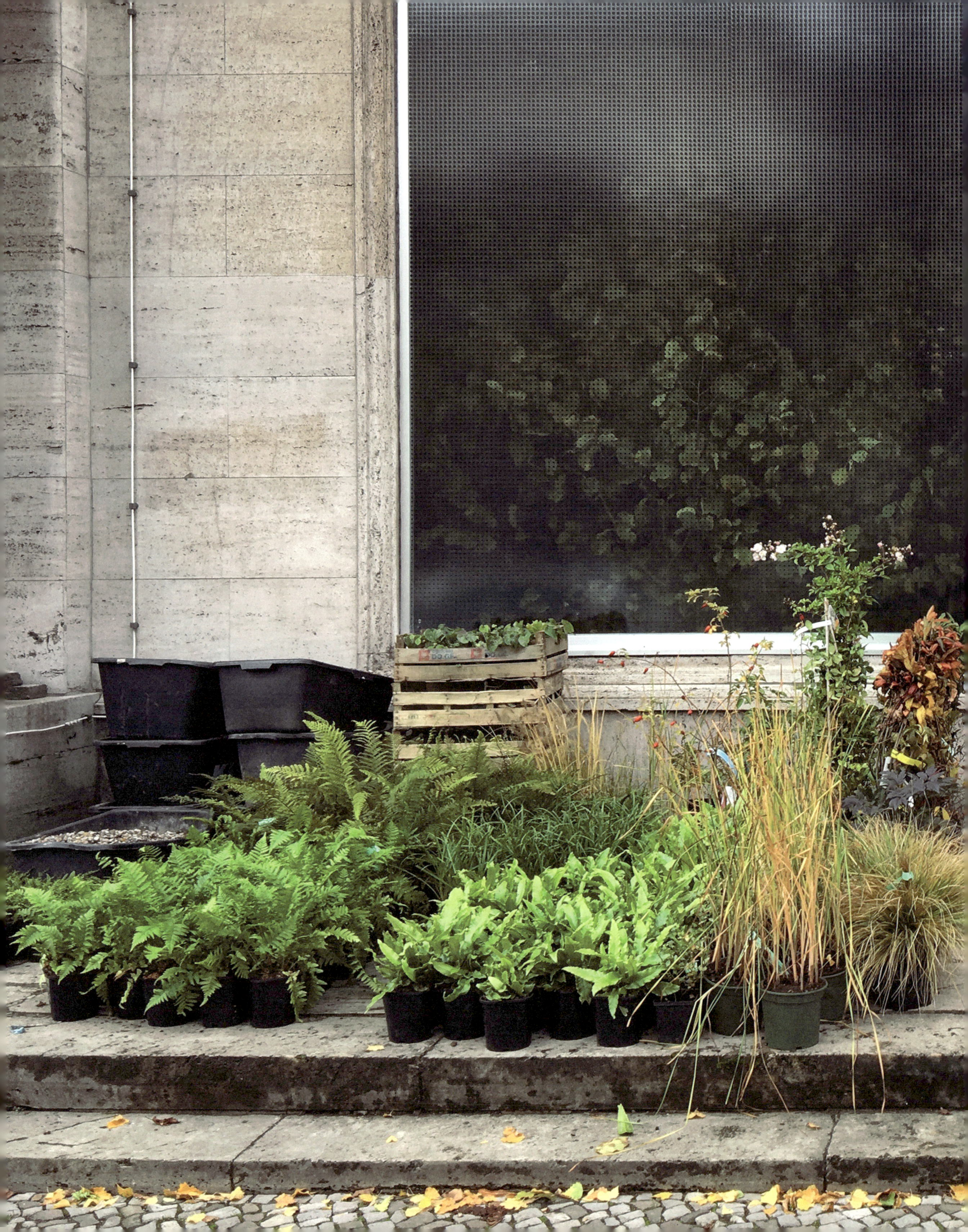